S0-AJD-626

JADWIGA

THE MACMILLAN COMPANY
NEW YORK · BOSTON · CHICAGO · DALLAS
ATLANTA · SAN FRANCISCO

MACMILLAN & CO., LIMITED
LONDON · BOMBAY · CALCUTTA
MELBOURNE

THE MACMILLAN COMPANY
OF CANADA, LIMITED
TORONTO

By Jan Matejko

DIMITRI OF GORAY PLEADS WITH JADWIGA TO SACRIFICE HER LOVE TO THE FUTURE GREATNESS OF POLAND

JADWIGA

POLAND'S GREAT QUEEN

BY

CHARLOTTE KELLOGG

WITH A PREFACE BY

IGNAZ JAN PADEREWSKI

AND AN INTRODUCTION BY

FRANK H. SIMONDS

NEW YORK

THE MACMILLAN COMPANY

1931

Set up and printed. Published October, 1931.

Printed in the United States of America by
J. J. LITTLE & IVES COMPANY, NEW YORK

To
L. S. M.

PREFACE

It is not an easy task to present to English or American readers the biography of a foreign Queen who ruled for a short time in a distant and unknown country, and who lived and died over five hundred years ago. A great deal of what we know about the most prominent figures of the Middle Ages, even in the older and highly civilized Western countries, is of a somewhat legendary character. A nimbus of popular poetry encircles the heads of the greatest among them. The admiring affection of generations erected for them enduring monuments in the hearts of multitudes always inclined to hero-worship.

In certain cases, however, the lack or scarcity of historical material, the insufficient knowledge of language or ambient conditions, make it extremely difficult to raise the veil of mystery hiding some unquestionable greatness and momentous merit. The taste of the public at large does hardly encourage such an effort. To the popular imagination, military valour appeals much more than charity or wisdom. A warrior destroying scores of human lives on a battle-field arouses more enthusiasm than the healer of as many wounds. And yet those, whom destiny has entrusted with the mission to preserve and strengthen the inviolable ties binding the present to the past, to reveal and enshrine the names of mankind's true benefactors, while challenging difficulties defy obstacles.

Jadwiga, Queen of Poland, was one of the purest and noblest creatures that had ever come out of God's hands. Upon her arrival in Cracow to take possession of the vacant throne, still a mere child, not quite fourteen years of age, she rapidly rose to the situation. Conscious of her enormous responsibilities, realizing that Poland, exhausted by incessant invasions, war, and domestic strife, desperately needed peace, she understood that nothing but a personal sacrifice could save the country. For her country's good, on the altar of duty, she made the supreme offering of her happiness. Though dearly beloved by her own people, she has been for centuries almost entirely unknown in the West of Europe. It evidently is the mission of an American lady, the authoress of this book, to acquaint the English-speaking public with that sublime figure.

After more than four centuries of eventful and glorious reigning the mighty Polish dynasty of Piast became extinct. The last direct offspring of that illustrious house, Casimir the Third, died in 1370 without leaving a male descendant. Among the members of the family's collateral branches, no one was worthy of occupying the throne vacated by such a ruler. Casimir's sagacity and justice, his tolerance and generosity, his keen foresight and constructive genius, had won for him—in spite of his occasionally excessive pacifism—the surname of "great." This verdict has been confirmed and maintained by posterity. A strong, remarkable woman, Casimir's sister, Elizabeth, Queen of Hungary, had already solved the problem of succession to the advantage of the Hungarian dynastic interests. With her assistance her husband, Charles Robert d'Anjou, King of Hungary, secured the Polish crown for their son, Louis, by a treaty concluded with Casimir in 1339.

The new King, far from possessing all the eminent qualities of his uncle, was a brilliant, highly educated man and he must have been a suitable, successful, beneficial ruler for the Hungarian people, because his grateful subjects called him "great" as well. For Poland, however, his reign was disastrous. Born of a Piast mother, Elizabeth of Poland, married to Elizabeth of Bosnia, whose mother was a Piast princess as well, he never took pains to learn the Polish language and never resided in Poland. From time to time, when certain of his projects could not be fully accomplished without the agreement of the Council of the Crown, he summoned the Polish notables to some distant Hungarian town or castle in order to obtain by perfidious promises, or even by violence, the necessary consent. Half French and half Polish, as to his blood, Louis constantly was under the intellectual and political influence of his German neighbours. Eagerly and ostentatiously he manifested his particular affection for the most bitter enemies of Poland, the Order of Teutonic Knights. The intermittent state of war between his Polish subjects and those rapacious German monks, the continuous attacks on the Polish border lands by the turbulent, pagan Lithuanians made but little impression upon a mind chiefly addicted to Hungary's aggrandizement and his own glory. The fertile province of Red Ruthenia, inherited by his uncle, Casimir, was arbitrarily detached by him from the Polish crown and incorporated into the realm of Hungary. No wonder that the news of his death was received in Poland with an intense feeling of relief.

For whatever wrong King Louis had done to Poland, the country and the people were richly repaid by his daughter Jadwiga. When, after two years of interregnum, after many vicissitudes, the Polish leaders succeeded at last in bringing her to Cracow for the coronation, she appeared on the horizon like a bright rainbow following a long and violent storm. Her beauty and charm, her precocious sagacity and tact, her modesty and piety and her valiant bearing conquered all hearts. Everybody was happy—except the young Queen.

In accordance with the customs prevailing at that time among royal houses, Jadwiga, when only seven years old, was betrothed to Prince William, hardly older than herself, son of Arch-Duke Leopold of Austria. The ceremony of betrothal ("the false marriage") took place, in 1378, at Haimburg with a great display of magnificence and pomp. It had to be followed by regular nuptials on the date of the couple's coming of age. Meanwhile the children spent a great deal of time together, at the splendid courts of Vienna or of Buda, and their companionship developed with the years into an ardent, passionate love. In her purity of heart, Jadwiga, already Queen of Poland, considered herself as indissolubly bound to William, and expected to celebrate the wedding-ceremony shortly after the coronation. But the Council of the Crown did not want to see a German prince sharing with Jadwiga the throne of Poland. They protested.

The resistance of the Polish magnates to Jadwiga's intent was the more stubborn as they had already opened negotiations with the delegates of another suitor of their young Queen, the Grand Duke of Lithuania, Yagiello. In their opinion the personal alliance of the two sovereigns would be of immense benefit to both countries and to civilization. Lithuania, still a small country at the beginning of the XIVth century, had suddenly grown into a mighty state, thanks to the military genius of her rulers, Gedymin and Olgierd, Yagiello's grandfather and father. Her territory now extended from the Baltic to the Black Sea. But the illiterate Yagiello and his aggressive, warlike Lithuanians were inveterate pagans, and they were looked upon as a barbarous people. Yagiello's delegates, two of his own brothers, offered, however, conditions which could not be rejected. They solemnly pledged that Yagiello, if he became King of Poland, would not only unite the vast Lithuanian territories with hers, restore and assist in regaining her lost lands, and with her defend the united countries against the aggressions of the Teutonic Knights and the Tartar hordes, but he would embrace Christianity with his whole people. What a bright prospect for an ever-menaced country! And what a tragedy for Jadwiga's heart!

Many a month she desperately fought against the merciless exigencies of the State. All her plans for a secret marriage, for abdication, for flight were frustrated by the ever-watchful though respectfully affectionate Council of the Crown. Seeing the futility of all her efforts, the distressed Queen tried to find solace and fortitude in the small chapel adjoining the ancient Cathedral of Cracow. One day, after long hours of fervent prayers, she heard—not unlike Sainte Jeanne d'Arc—"voices" from above calling upon her to perform a royal duty. . . . She listened. With the humility of a pious, medieval soul, she obeyed. For the safety of her country and people, for the triumph of Christianity, she forsook her dreams of childhood, her desires of youth. She married Yagiello.

Thus came a miracle unique in the annals of Europe. Following the sacrifice of a young Queen, two inimical countries, two ever-warring nations, concluded a lasting peace. They joined together their destinies. They formed a federation, a union which lasted undisturbed over four hundred years and even survived Poland's partitions.

True to his word, Yagiello faithfully fulfilled all his promises. Within a short time, by persuasion, by command or by force, indeed he converted his whole people to the Catholic religion. There was at first much discontent, of course, but the simple, naïve people, seeing that the destruction of their idols, the killing of their sacred serpents, the burning of their holy oaks had not been followed by the collapse of the world, nor punished by any other minor calamity, peacefully accepted the new creed, and soon became a civilized nation. The Western culture applied to a fertile soil did not fail to produce abundant fruit. A great many distinguished Polish writers, poets, scientists, musicians, statesmen, heroic captains, of purely Lithuanian or Slavic stock, were born in the old Yagiellonian dominions.

As to Yagiello, gifted as he was, discreetly influenced by his in so many ways superior, though much younger, consort, he did not lose time in adapting himself to the new conditions. A born ruler, wise and just, with his natural impetuosity considerably softened by a profound religious feeling, he easily adopted Western, Polish ideals and swiftly turned into a great constitutional King. In recognition of his noble character, of his absolute honesty and loyalty, Jadwiga appointed him as her only successor. The dynasty he founded was one of the most illustrious that ever ruled on earth. Under the reign of the Yagiellonian

House Poland attained the summit of her prosperity and power.

When looking back at Jadwiga's distressingly short life, one cannot help wondering at her achievements. As a girl of sixteen, after having heroically given up her personal happiness, she realizes the profound truth of one of her teacher's, Scribe John's saying: "Life's bright objective is the complete gift of itself to others." Since that moment all her marvellous gifts are wholeheartedly dedicated to State affairs and to the welfare of her people. Endowed with indomitable energy, with an astounding instinct for statesmanship, she takes an active part in every deliberation of the Council of the Crown. Her sense of justice is so strong, her judgment so sound, and her influence so great that both the King and the nobles cannot but bow before her opinion. During one of Yagiello's frequent journeys, when only seventeen years of age, she decides to march at the head of a small army of Polish knights into Red Ruthenia, so willfully annexed by her own father, King Louis. Everywhere enthusiastically received by the population, she definitely restores that rich province to the Polish Crown.

This was her only military operation which did not, however, involve the loss of one single human life. In everything else she was true to her lofty mission as an apostle of peace. She acted as a peacemaker between Yagiello's brother, Skirgello, and his cousin, the ambitious, adventurous, and remarkably gifted Prince Witold; she reconciled several other very quarrelsome members of Yagiello's numerous family; she practically pacified Great-Poland by putting an end to the long, implacable feud between the two powerful clans of Grzymala and Nalencz.

Mindful of the ties that had been binding her father, King Louis, to the Order of Teutonic Knights, Jadwiga did all she could to prevent an open war with the greedy and unrelentingly aggressive monks. She saw the terrible suffering that must desolate her land once the Order's and Poland's forces were in battle. While people blessed her for having saved them from that war thus far, Yagiello, troubled without respite by unceasing assaults and plundering of the border lands, could hardly control his impatience. But Jadwiga remained inflexible in her determination to preserve peace. She was aware of all the wrong those pioneers of the "Drang nach Osten" were doing her country. She knew that they were already planning a partition of Poland, and yet, hoping against hope, she yielded to the King's and the Council's wishes and went with a gorgeous retinue to personally confer with the Grand Master of Marienburg, the capital of the Order. The conferences proved to be of no avail. The demands of the monks were so exorbitant that the Queen interrupted further discussions and, in a voice in which the note of prophecy mingled with bitterness and indignation, said: "So long as I live the Crown will endure your iniquities, but after my death the chastisement of Heaven will fall upon you and then inevitable war will consummate your ruin."

And, indeed, eleven years after Jadwiga's death, Yagiello, at the head of the Polish and Lithuanian armies, inflicted upon the Order of Teutonic Knights, the 15th of July, 1410, a crushing, decisive defeat.

Jadwiga's generosity was inexhaustible. While bountifully helping the poor of her country, she built numerous hospitals, schools, convents, and churches. She established many scholarships for the Lithuanian youth at the University of Prague. But the principal object of her affection and solicitude was the University of Cracow, founded by her grand-uncle, Casimir, in 1364. During her lifetime she bought several houses in order to provide the grounds to surround that institution and to permit the extension of its buildings. In her last will she directed "one half of the proceeds from the sale of all I have, jewels, clothes, ornaments, possessions of every kind, I leave to the University of Cracow and the other half to be divided among the poor." Thus, thanks to the thoughtful and munificent bequest of the Queen, the University of Cracow was enabled to become one of the important centers of knowledge in old Europe.

Jadwiga's private life was marked by many cruel bereavements. She had to mourn nearly all those who were dear to her heart. By a few days only she survived her little daughter and died in 1399, leaving a memory that seems to be imperishable.

The people of Poland, who almost unanimously

consider Jadwiga as a saint, will be deeply grateful to Mrs. Vernon Kellogg for having paid such a beautiful and glowing tribute to their cherished Queen. In the graphic and captivating narrative which follows these lines the readers will find a true picture of a wonderful life. With the painstaking erudition of an historian, with the imagination of a poet, with manly vigor and womanly fondness of detail, Mrs. Vernon Kellogg undertook an arduous task and brought it to a successful end. She loves Jadwiga. And a work of love is bound to succeed.

I. J. Paderewski

INTRODUCTION

THE romance of Jadwiga and Jagiello is so moving in itself, that it must seem a piece of unforgivable pedantry to undertake to load it with historical incumbrances. And yet, aside from the union of Ferdinand and Isabella, it may be questioned whether any royal marriage in Europe ever had more far-reaching consequences, as it is clear that none has bestowed a graver inheritance of disturbing problems upon contemporary mankind. For, if today European peace is troubled by the overshadowing issue of the Polish Corridor and by the dispute over Vilno, these are the direct results of the wedding upon Wawel Hill five centures and a half ago.

Between the two royal marriages, those of Ferdinand and Isabella and of Jadwiga and Jagiello, the parallel is also striking. The union of Castile and Aragon had, as its immediate consequence, the expulsion of the Moors from Spain and as its eventual result the launching of Spain upon her great period of European power and American empire. And, precisely in the same fashion, the union of Poland and Lithuania proved the prelude to the breaking of the power of the Teutonic Knights upon the field of Tannenberg and was the beginning of three centuries of Polish greatness culminating in the exploit of John Sobieski under the walls of Vienna.

Thus, in a very real sense the issue of this marriage, which Mrs. Kellogg has described in her vivid and fascinating chapters, was Poland, that Poland which was destined for long centuries to be the soldier of Christianity and the servant of western culture in all of the east of Europe from the Baltic to the Black Sea and from the Warthe to the Dnieper.

Moreover, if one is to understand the Poland of today, which, at the very dawn of its renaissance resumed its ancient mission by breaking the invasive force of Bolshevism before the gates of Warsaw, the first essential is to know something of those centuries of greatness and achievement which extend from the first Jagiello at least to the death of Sobieski.

Only thus can one measure the unanimous and irresistible impulse which drove the Poles to reclaim that ancient window of their race upon the sea, which is the Corridor, to reoccupy their second capital, the Vilno of Jagiello, and to defend Lvov, which has been the Verdun of Poland in the southeast for untold centuries.

What the world had too easily forgotten in the long generations of Polish captivity was not merely that Poland had once been a great power, but also that even in slavery the Poles remained in tradition, in numbers, above all in spirit, a great people, certain, once their prison doors were opened, to seek not merely their old liberty but their historic unity, that unity described in the Proclamation of Lublin in 1569 in language which the revolutionaries of 1792 borrowed to announce the French Republic as "one and indivisible." And this Proclamation of Lublin was no more than the reaffirmation of the union achieved through the marriage of Jadwiga and Jagiello.

The western frontiers of the state created by the union of Poland and Lithuania were definitely fixed by the Second Peace of Thorn, a quarter of a century before Columbus set sail upon his first voyage. They endured right down to the eve of the American Revolution and were restored with but inconsiderable changes, by the Treaty of Versailles, largely through the uncompromising insistence of Woodrow Wilson.

Today, for twenty millions of Poles these frontiers constitute not boundaries enclosing provinces and populations but the limits of the living body of Poland. They are symbols of a territorial unity older than that of any other European people, great or small, which, before the United States achieved national existence, had endured twice as long as the span between Washington and Hoover.

And the permanent service of Mrs. Kellogg's book lies precisely in the fact that she has not merely provided an authentic portrait of a noble and romantic figure and a fascinating picture of the pageantry of mediæval ceremony but has also seized upon one of the great and illuminating events in the history of a people, whose liberation was not impossibly the greatest single result of the World War and whose future certainly constitutes the most perplexing and dangerous of all pending problems in Post-War Europe.

FRANK H. SIMONDS.

Louisiana Purchase,
November 4, 1930.

ACKNOWLEDGMENTS

THE author wishes to acknowledge her indebtedness to the following persons for their generous assistance in her research: in Krakow—first, to Professor Jean Dabrowski, of Krakow University; then to Director Adam Chmiel of the old archives building, Professor Roman Dyboski, Doctor Stanislas Tomkowicz, and Miss Marja Slomczanka. In Warsaw, to Professors Oskar Halecki and Szymon Askenazy, and to Doctor Janusz Pajewski, of Warsaw University. In Budapest, to Count Kuno Klebelsberg, Minister of Education; Doctor Ida Bobula; Doctor Dennis Janossy, Doctor Kalman Lux. In Vienna, to Doctor Lothar Gross, Director of Archives. In Königsberg, to Doctor Max Hein, Director of Archives, and Doctor Forstreuter, his assistant. In Vilno, to Doctor Stanislas Lorenz, Conservator of Monuments.

In addition to this scholarly assistance, the author is grateful to many others for friendly aid in her quest. She would mention especially Reverend Coleman Nevils, S. J., President of Georgetown University, Washington, D. C.; Mr. Tytus Filipowicz, Polish Ambassador in Washington; Count Lazlo Szechenyi, Hungarian Minister in Washington; Doctor Herbert Putnam, Librarian of the Congressional Library,

Washington; Professor J. Strohl of Zurich; Mr. Butler Wright, American Minister in Budapest; and Mr. Mical Sokolnicki, Chief of the Historical Division, the Ministry of Foreign Affairs, Warsaw; and to Mrs. Mary Roberts Rinehart.

CONTENTS

CONTENTS

JADWIGA

JADWIGA: POLAND'S GREAT QUEEN

CHAPTER I

The False Marriage

At Buda, beside the Danube, in the blue June of 1378, Jadwiga was still but a girl of five; though the exuberant development of children of southeastern Europe made her look several years older. Tall for her age, her body was nevertheless firm and round, and her dancing blue eyes said that beneath her mature mien she was merry as a lark. Thick sunny hair rippled back from a wide forehead and she had a dimple in her firm little chin which had already inspired many a teasing song. From the time she had been permitted to see visitors at her father's court her radiant personality had won them.

So it was not alone interest in the incalculable political importance of the event to be celebrated this month that led cavalcades from the four quarters of the western world to focus on the hill town of Hainburg on the Austro-Hungarian frontier. Not alone interest in Habsburgs of Vienna or Anjevins of Buda; but also a desire actually to see the little princess whose beauty and charm had already caught the imagination of Europe.

Three years had passed since Archduke Leopold III

of Austria and King Louis the Great of Hungary and Poland had signed the first document recording the betrothal of Louis' third daughter, Princess Jadwiga, to Leopold's son, Crown Prince William. And during none of that time had King Louis felt the alliance sufficiently secure. In unstable Europe plot followed plot. So, with Leopold, he had arranged an impressive confirmation of the pact, and set the gothic Cathedral crowning Hainburg hill and the first month of '78 as time and place. The mediæval rite called the "false marriage" was to be the cementing ceremony. Louis was impatient for the day when he could confidently rely on the growing Habsburg strength for support in the west; when the Danube would be but a gleaming ribbon uniting the fertile territories of the two patrimonies.

In those days people gathered long in advance of a celebration. First, because festivities were life to them, their preliminaries as well as their climaxes. Then, what with uncertainties of weather and bad, unlighted roads, of time consumed by night stops and visiting en route, and the difficulty of finding lodgings and viewpoints once a city was full, it was well not to skimp the allotment of travel days. Since early January there had been so much activity in Hainburg that it was difficult to pass at the gates; every bed in the monasteries and hospitable houses and inns and haylofts was in use and tents dotted the hill.

When the Habsburg family arrived they and their shining retinue were given a resounding welcome.

The broad-shouldered, bearded, soldier-duke Leopold, though neither so picturesque nor so popular as his brother Duke Albert, was yet recognized as a courageous and promising ruler. This was a great day for his house. As the crowd watched him and his Italian wife Vividia and their eight year old son, Prince William, move up along the hill road toward the royal quarters, there was added to the customary clamor of greeting a noisy note of appreciation of the unusual importance of the event their coming heralded.

As soon as they had disappeared within the chateau, the multi-colored throng on the hilltop turned to watch the eastward road on which the second royal cavalcade must soon appear. From the glitter of ceremonial vestment and mantle one easily singled out prelates, government officials and their wives, and ambassadors, and among these especially the "White Cape" envoys of the northern Teutonic Knights. Blue robes of Cistercian monks, black of Benedictines and brown robes of Franciscans wound like a variegated ribbon through the ranks. Knights who had not yet removed their armor, rich merchants from as far away as the thriving Hanse cities of Lubeck and Danzig, landowners with their people, some in coats of mail, others in shaggy furs—all pressed eagerly for positions commanding the approach from Hungary. The Magyars, who according to heralds had been journeying many days, were coming from Visegrád their favorite capital, some thirty miles nearer Austria than Buda. This expectant, mobile multitude was accustomed to pageants, but on the continent scarcely another spectacle would match today's. Did not the kingdoms and principalities of the Great Louis cover the half of Europe?

Before long, on the road which wound with the river valley through the sparkling hill country, the gleaming line swung into sight. Following the outriders was a horse easily recognized from afar, caparisoned in flowing silk of the broad red and white stripes, of the Árpáds, the Magyar Kings whom Louis' father, Charles Robert, succeeded. King Louis rode splendidly erect in his high saddle, wearing a magnificent helmet topped by an ostrich head holding a horseshoe in its mouth and flanked by ostrich plumes. Armies of Naples and Venice and the Balkans well might waver as with the cry "Hurta, Hurta, Hungerland!" the Anjevin hurled his troops upon them. Men found in his courage their example. From mouth to mouth had gone the story of his having leaped into a swollen stream to save a drowning soldier whom he had ordered to ford it.

Today the king as well as his horse wore the Árpád colors; they striped the silken mantle covering his coat of mail, whose upper folds hung straight to those spreading from beneath the saddle. One of the things the watchers wished particularly to see was this famous saddle, picturing in carved ivory insets those victories over the Turks which had led Pope Innocent III to name the zealous Louis, Rex Christianissimus. Let Turk and Bogomil and every other heretic outside the fold, beware this son of the Church.

The great gilded coach drawn by six horses followed behind the king. In it sat the two Elizabeths, Louis' clever mother whom he had made queen regent of Poland, and the dark-eyed Bosnian wife he had married chiefly because he loved her. The young princesses, Mary and Jadwiga, rode with them. As the line neared, many recognized familiar figures of the Hungarian Court. Handsome archbishop Dimitri of Estergom, clad in the spreading purple of Rome, and agile-minded Nicolas Gara, first man of the realm, rode near the king. There was chief Justice Jacob; Queen Elizabeth's physician, the Bishop of Veszprem; and the king's physician, Doctor John Radlica; Scribe John of Aprod, his historian-secretary, and a host of other officials and knights. Along all the length of the procession of horses and supply wagons—and there were many such wagons carrying wardrobes and gifts, food and beds, and other necessities for visiting—color was lifted high by plume and pennant and silver horn.

The second arrival on the hilltop was announced by a second prolonged fanfare of trumpets and by shouts of, "Long live the Great Louis! Long live the Queen Mother, Queen Elizabeth and the princesses! Long live Princess Jadwiga!" Here was a ruler who satisfied the popular conception of royal appearance. His commanding stature, splendidly curled hair and beard, the flashing sweep of his blue eyes in which burned the fires of both warrior and mystic, so held the gaze that one scarcely noticed a drooping shoulder.

It was moving in itself merely to see this family together; in all the courts of Europe there was none more devoted. Not that such devotion escaped the customary jibes of sharp tongues. Many attractive girls had been educated at the court of Louis' father—Anna of Silesia, Dorothy of Bulgaria, Margaret of Luxemburg—but the quick-eyed Louis had seen only one. It was common knowledge that in his impetuous love for buoyant Elizabeth of Bosnia, he had won her as wife before the marriage ceremony. And that his vigorous mother, had it not been for the strength of her son's passion, would have urged the guilty girl to enter a convent there to pray and repent during the rest of her life. But that was long ago! In fact, Louis and Elizabeth were this month celebrating their twenty-fifth wedding anniversary. Today people whispered, "The strong king is not able to move without first consulting a petticoat." "When the Pope wants something of King Louis, he first wins the interest of one of the Elizabeths." Others added that though the younger queen preserved a perfect poise, secretly her husband's dependence on her mother-in-law's superior intelligence and experience left her far from calm.

However, there was no evidence today of anything but accord, as amidst further shouting and singing, the dynamic, gray-haired old lady whose blue eyes laughed an intense joy in life and her darkly lovely daughter-in-law led the two princesses through the arched portal of the chateau. There, both Austrians and Hungarians were to pass the night in festivities and in preparing for the approaching ceremony; while outside their people, gathered about the tents, gave rein to their own lusty anticipation of the morrow.

The Habsburg eagle was as yet but a fledgling, learning from Archduke Leopold and his brother Albert to spread its wings. Leopold had much to discuss with his neighbor, and first, their Italian policies. In the dynastic game of both, as indeed in that of most European monarchs, Italy, without a central ruler, and throbbing with a vitality that was blossoming in hitherto undreamed of beauty, was an ever-beckoning field of exploitation. As neighbors of Italy, the Austrian archduke and the king of the Magyars had the start of others in that game of ambition and greed. At this time too, Leopold was particularly troubled by the menace to Austrian expansion of the growing spirit of independence and democracy in the Swiss alpine regions. For on a continent where the people were yet feeble and inexpressive, and where rulers followed the common program of mailed aggrandizement, the Swiss were integrating themselves. They must be stopped.

And King Louis had much on his mind. Under his illustrious father, who had carried the French Anjevin line from Naples to Buda, Hungary's territories spread far and were well-governed. Charles Robert had reformed its systems of defense and agriculture and finance, and made his mark as an administrator. Moreover, he had turned his dream of securing the Polish crown into a reality. For after his marriage with the clever sister of the Piast King, Casimir the Great of Poland, Casimir had become interested in their son Louis, and setting aside the northern Piast branch, had named his promising nephew his successor. Which had complicated Louis' task; for to rule as absentee King of Poland, even with so capable a person as his mother acting as regent, was an undertaking bristling with difficulties.

Nor did uncertainties in the north help matters in the south, where Louis had continually to watch Venice, if Hungary was to maintain her hold on glowing Dalmatian lands. Venice, opulent, radiant, lifting her facades of Istrian marble from the uniting waters, was glorious in war as in peace. In marrying Elizabeth Kotromanić, daughter of the powerful Ban of Bosnia, Louis had hoped to strengthen his arm in the south, but he had not found in Bosnia the support he had sought.

And Naples! He had conducted expedition after expedition against Naples; primarily to avenge the murder of his brother Andrew, for he believed Andrew's wife, Queen Joanna, to be the instigator of that crime. At one time he had conquered much of the little kingdom, and his goal, the union of Naples with Hungary, seemed assured. But a terrible earthquake and pestilence and a general feeling against him had forced his return to Hungary. Nor had he since then, despite victories, reached that goal. He was now playing a game of watchful diplomacy.

Of shuddering concern to Leopold as to himself, since both Vienna and Buda were Mohammedan objectives, was the threat of another Turkish invasion. Any heretic could fan to a flame Louis' religious zeal, but he concentrated his defensive and retaliatory effort on the Turk. Could man ever forget 1360 and '71 and other dread dates? The Church and the whole of western Europe looked to Hungary to save it from the ever looming repetition of these cataclysms.

While he was riding toward Hainburg, King Louis had been looking backward—something he indulged in rarely. During the first thirty years of his reign he seemed to have been engaged in a continuous military expedition. He had lost much blood. His body was wound scarred. Once in a siege in the south, when an enemy arrow had imbedded itself in his leg, and after his knights, pulling and twisting, had in thirteen attempts failed to extract it, he had yet managed to climb again to his saddle and lead his troops to victory. Always he had had to carry his life in his hands. Small wonder that he wished now to rest on the thought of strong alliances with neighboring powers.

He had not too enthusiastically engaged his sweet-faced, gentle Mary, who was four years older than Jadwiga, to young Prince Sigismund, son of the Holy

Roman Emperor Charles IV and the granddaughter of Louis' Polish Uncle, King Casimir. Sigismund was heir to the mark of Brandenburg. Through his second daughter, Catherine, he had hoped one day to attach Naples; but four years ago Catherine died. Now, of primal importance was this union with Austria. After his death, Mary and Sigismund would rule Poland and Brandenburg. And under Jadwiga and William, Hungary and Austria would be united.

Moreover, Louis was thinking far beyond matters which he this night discussed with Leopold. He faced increasingly, of late, the fundamental question as to what life, after all, was most worth while. In this age given to unceasing warfare, he yet never forgot that he was a lineal descendant of Saint Louis of France. He could not escape the strange longing to slip out of the steel armor which was one symbol of his century, and under the monk's cape which was another symbol. Possessing enormous powers—he ruled practically as absolute monarch—he was torn between his ambition to make the Hungarian court the first in Europe, and a desire to renounce that court and the world altogether. Who could tell, perhaps this Hainburg ceremony might prove a gateway to the withdrawal of which he thus dreamed. . . .

The following morning while the hill bells shook the clear air, people hurried to the Cathedral, where Austrian and Hungarian archbishops in pontifical robes stiff with gold, were to officiate. There the flood of candlelight reflected from altar crucifix and chalice was now caught by farther cuirass and jewelled necklace. As the royal families passed from the sacristy to the sanctuary, and the crowd pressed for a better viewpoint, clanking of metal and rustling of brocade mingled with the music.

Little William and Jadwiga, already accustomed to think of themselves not only as playmates, but as knight and lady destined for each other, had advanced to this next step quite naturally. But once within the dim Cathedral, in the presence of the powerful of two realms, they sensed with a kind of awe that something of deeper import than they understood was happening to them. As they advanced up the closely lined aisle toward the altar the great company leaned forward.

Warm glances approved the slim, erect boy prince of Austria in his red silk mantle, on which the Habsburg eagle was heavily embroidered in gold. There was much sweetness in the expression of the blue eyes and delicacy in the finely moulded face. One wished, however, that he were less frail—the young shoulders seemed not yet ready to support heavy mantles.

But as always, eyes turned quickly to the bride, on this occasion a bride in symbol only. What a picture she made, in her heaven-hued robe flowered with lilies of France, her golden hair rippling over her shoulders. Like a wind running across the water ran a murmur of admiration. The glowing warmth of her skin and vivid blue of her eyes called forth many an enthusiastic simile. "Lovely as a rose," "sweet and strong as a young fir tree," "a true lily of France," was this little princess.

At the altar the archbishops received them, and as they knelt on crimson velvet cushions under a cloud of incense, the solemn ritual began. At its conclusion, while organ notes and chanting echoed in the high vaulting, Archbishop Dimitri joined their hands in sacred and inviolable pledge. The great lords of Austria and Hungary and their neighbors looking on, tried to measure the potentialities of this hour for Europe, and the clergy its meaning to Rome—not the least active in speculation being those emissaries from the Baltic coast, the white-caped German Knights of the Cross.

Many keenly watched the two Elizabeths. For it was known that this day of triumph for one, was a day of defeat for the other. The queen mother strongly favored the betrothal, but the queen had from the beginning obdurately opposed an alliance with German Austria. However, neither the vivacious countenance of Jadwiga's Polish grandmother, reputed for her royal wisdom, nor the darkly beautiful face of her Bosnian mother, to whom love was the omnipotent force in life, revealed anything which might help to forecast the future.

The religious phase of the ceremony over, all rendered homage and added good wishes to the archbishops' blessings and then the royal suites escorted Jadwiga and William to the chateau. There, at the betrothal banquet, contributions from the game-filled forests of Austria, orchards of the Danube Valley, and wine cellars of Italy and France added Nature's exuberant approval of this pact. Musicians and jesters now had their opportunity. There was no end of merry-making—some one had even brought a trained bear into the hall. The young pair, glad to let solemnity slip from their shoulders, gave themselves with joyous zest to the feasting and dancing.

They had not yet exhausted these delights, when they were initiated into the more extraordinary part of the celebration. They were led to the nuptial chamber, told to lie upon a splendid bed and, as the silken cover was drawn over them, to kiss each other. A warm-blooded child of the southeast, Jadwiga was never to forget this and other symbolic rites prefiguring her true marriage with William, when he would be fourteen. This was an age of early majorities and early marriages; Isabel of France had been married at eight to Richard of England.

So seriously was the false marriage considered that legal arrangements were made for the inheritance of the dots (Jadwiga's was 200,000, William's 300,000 florins), in case of the death of either child. No mere will of an emperor now could break the pact; it could henceforth be annulled only by the Pope himself.

Churches and convents were already asking for the future wedding clothes of this prospective king and queen; for it was customary to give them away. "If you have promised your upper garments, then give us your under clothes," one Order had written, "or your girdle and golden stirrups and spurs." Magnificently embroidered mass vestments had been made from the marriage robes of Jadwiga's parents.

And still King Louis' mind was not at rest. Before the contracting ink was dry he was planning further safeguards, wondering how he could add surety to surety. He would continue to have bishops and cardinals and cities add their signatures to attest the inviolability of the alliance. And simultaneously Queen Elizabeth was deciding that she would send as a gift to Pope Urban VI, a gold crown worth 20,000 florins. She knew him to be the enemy of William's father, who was supporting the false pope at Avignon!

After such a prolonged appeal to their young imaginations and emotions, was it strange that in this romantic age, William and Jadwiga, as they grew older should look upon their own as the most perfect love story? They were prince and princess, soon to be peerless knight and damsel of matchless beauty and virtue, soon to be king and queen. Yet underneath all with which the pomp of courts and glamor of chivalry had invested them, they were just happy boy and girl comrades.

CHAPTER II

Together at the Austrian Court

The stream of inheritance had already laid on little Jadwiga's threshold the complex total of its gift. Daily, now, environment was determining her development within those inexorable lines already set. Some of the greatest names in the world of letters were united with those of her Anjevin ancestors, one of whom was able to say to Dante in Il Paradiso, "Sufficiently thou lovedst me." Through her father, what mysteriously selected, long-carried seeds were sown in her blood? What measure of the imaginative fervor, the mystic rapture, of Saint Louis had she received? Had she her father's capacities? His vigor? Perhaps his excessive ardor? For while King Louis filled the years with great accomplishments, at times an almost fanatical zeal left dark stains upon them.

From the Piasts of Poland—her great uncle Casimir and her grandmother Elizabeth—what heritage of mental and physical virility was hers? From her gay, warm-hearted mother, what capacity for loving? And from all, what ancestral sense of race and of dynastic and religious duty, to hold her ship steady on a stormy course? Already, some thought that they could read, at least partially, answers to these questions.

One of the important influences of these impressionable years immediately following the Hainburg ceremony came out of Austria. After the formal betrothal, according to custom, each child was to live for some time with the family of the other, partly as hostage, partly as pupil. This took Jadwiga to Austria and William to Hungary. However, the traditional sojourn was often interrupted by exchanges of visits. Far from Buda and Visegrád, and separated from her loved comrade for weeks, or months, Jadwiga was all uncontrolled joyousness when William returned to Vienna to be for a time with his parents. The fact that he came now as the messenger of her own family made him doubly dear to her.

In Vienna they chattered German instead of Hungarian. Fortunately, there, they were not so much under the guidance of William's father, Leopold, and his mother (a daughter of the cruel Viscontis of Milan) as under that of William's dispossessed uncle, picturesque Duke Albert III. Leopold's appetite for kingship was more typical of his age than Albert's. The peace-lover, Albert was called, though the title did not imply lack of courage. He wore his hair in a cue; indeed, was credited with having started that mode in France.

Albert found pleasure in superintending the education of his protégés. And better still, he gave them much personal companionship. He talked to them glowingly of ships and mariners and the compass and of the thrilling adventures of the rich merchants of the great Hanseatic League—these were tales rivaling their favorite stories of Marco Polo. He reviewed Austria's expeditions against Venice, and described the beauty of that island city. He painted with terrifying vividness the peril of Islam, for ever since, a few years earlier, the Ottoman Turks had penetrated to the heart of old Servia, that peril had been the European obsession. He talked of Asia that lay under a cloud of conjecture and fable. Of the Tatar, Techtamisch, who two years ago had been made Khan by Timur the Lame, and might with the Golden Horde at any time take Moscow and sweep like a tide from Russian steppes westward. He talked of his retreats, when at times he withdrew to a monastery to pray and sing canticles. He introduced them to birds and roses and streams in the gardens of his favorite country estate, and, most important of all, to his baby son, who was the delight of his days. Altogether he captivated their young minds and hearts.

This was the period of early gothic in Austria; noise of hammers and chisels filled the air. The Habsburgs were laying the foundations of the beautiful capital Vienna was to become. The fine Minorite Church already thrilled the city, Saint Stephen's Cathedral was growing. The children were greatly interested in the busts of himself and his wife which Duke Albert was having set above one of its portals.

He was an ardent student and was busy creating schools and zoological parks, having exquisite religious manuscripts executed, botanies illustrated—trying to find out all that was known in science and art. He enjoyed especially lingering with the young people in front of the wooden cabinet which was his library. It would have been difficult to find more richly laden shelves in any other chateau in Europe. Sitting before them Jadwiga and William held in their hands and turned the pages of Albert's treasured book of the four Evangelists, written in purest gold and exquisitely illustrated. They could have had no more inspiring teacher.

When pleasantly left to their own devices, they found the fortress-palace a place of inexhaustible interest. If there were not other more important tours of investigation to be made there were always those within the chateau itself. These might lead to the head kitchen master, or the silver room man, the cellar scribe, the lights man, the head stable man, to the man who knocked on the doors so that all would go to sleep, to musicians and gardeners—all of whom inhabited a world of alluring suggestion.

Their favorite singer on the court programs was a chevalier of great influence, the beloved poet Suchenwirt, who was a frequent sojourner, too, at the Hungarian court, and knew many lands and peoples. Indeed, scarcely a week passed without the arrival of some singing chronicler, who had already been Jadwiga's friend at Visegrád. Such visitors always offered especial entertainment to the young princesses.

And with what comparative ease men travelled, despite poor roads. Happily, too, Latin was a true international language, and a common language was of far greater importance than roads free of dust and mud. It was only in travelling slowly that one could learn; long journeys on horse and on foot, and time spent enjoying the hospitality of convent and court, gave opportunity for discussion and reflection. With printing yet unknown, there was a constant call to discover facts for oneself. Moreover, the continual travelling was born of a deeper restlessness. Europe had not yet settled down after the Crusades and great ethnic bodies were still feeling their way to geographic permanence.

What a fascinating earth to live on, despite the fact that so much of it was still undiscovered—for another century oceans were still to hide the Americas. A world inheriting the civilization of Asia and Africa, and Greece and Rome, did not seem limited; many epochs which to us are closed books were for Jadwiga's people richly written. They thought not in terms of parochial frontiers, but in those of the Catholic Church, ever spreading toward universal boundaries. Hungarian Cistercian, or Franciscan, was brother to his brothers in cloisters in other lands and exchanged visits with them. This religious orientation, joined to the amazing political conception of the Holy Roman Empire, made the developing world a place of boundless horizons. Though the prestige of each was waning, the papacy and the empire were still the two powerful omnipresent influences of the time. However, beneath this specious unity, surging up from the bottom was the new growth, which was blossoming in vernacular languages and in the lusty individuality of the cities.

This, then, was a world in movement, a world detached from any fixed abode. Did a teacher win success in a certain town? Students gathered from far and near to sit at his feet. Was such an event as the Hainburg ceremony about to be celebrated? Pilgrim bands of every description set forth to witness it. If one felt the necessity of a comforting sense of stability, he found it in the thought of the eternal home awaiting him. Indeed, had somebody asked Jadwiga where her father, the king, lived, she could not have answered in one word. For Louis' "homes" dotted the half of Europe. He preferred, to be sure, his Visegrád palaces above the river in summer, and those at the lower capital, Buda, in winter. But he might be found making long sojourns at any one of a dozen of his seats he had scattered about the kingdom, holding a council here or a court there, signing a document far from the capital. And all this was quite aside from the far-flung military and crusading exploits which might lead him on expeditions against northern Lithuania or southern Venice or to wars in the Balkans which would last for months.

At the Vienna court, as elsewhere, there was a current events department. Suchenwirt was at once poet and pressman. The young people delighted in his thrusts at knights "who don't go home until morning and sleep over mass time!" Legends of the past, news of the contemporary day equally crowded his narration. Two contemporary happenings filled the world with their repercussions. All Europe fixed its attention on the recent deaths of Pope Gregory XI, and of Charles IV, Kaiser of the Holy Roman Empire. And now Christians, in a church divided against itself, watched with conflicting interest the strange drama in progress at Rome. In the hope of silencing the two rival popes who were thundering anathemas at each other, Saint Catherine of Sienna had gone to the Holy City, and without money, but with secretaries and seven Sisters of Penance, had taken up her abode in the Via di Papa. From there, while she exhorted the new Pope Urban VI, to curb the violence of his temper, she launched her eloquent appeals to all Christian nations to turn their backs on Avignon and the "false pope" Clement VII and to support Rome and Urban VI. Especially she was hoping to win over the notorious Queen Joanna of Naples, an ally of Clement. And to that end she had written Jadwiga's father who hated Joanna:

"Much good will result from your coming hither. Perhaps the true cause will triumph without the use of physical force, and the deluded Queen may be rescued from her obstinate perversion either by fear or by love. You are well aware how the Christ has spared her hitherto, being unwilling to deprive her actually of that which by her conduct she has forfeited. He has awaited her repentance out of consideration of you and your family."

In response King Louis and Queen Elizabeth had sent Urban a magnificent present of jewels to make up for the loss of those which the cardinals had carried off to Avignon.

But, children as they were, William and Jadwiga at Vienna were far more interested in tales of war, in stories of the still unforgotten Crusades. Most enthralling, too, were the dramatic recitals of that Crusade which belonged not to older days but to their own time. They sat absorbed hour after hour while Suchenwirt recounted some adventure of the Teutonic Knights, soldiers of Christ and members of an order which, having early made the great adventure in the Holy Land and later retreated sullenly, sword in hand, before the Ottoman infidel, had now removed from the brilliant East to the dark and gloomy North.

They wore casques tufted with peacock feathers and long white capes emblazoned with black crosses, and had their chief strongholds at Königsberg and Marienburg near the Baltic shore. From these fortress-palaces they conducted one glorious crusade after another into the country of the Lithuanians, that powerful people who still worshipped the god of thunder and the sacred serpent. Their possessions, lying northeast and southeast of Poland, had been vastly increased in recent years by their leader, Duke Olgierd, called "Terror of the Russ." Jadwiga's father had gone on a crusade against them, in memory of which his royal sword still hung in the great hall at Königsberg.

Only last year Duke Albert himself had started forth, accompanied by two thousand men on horseback, to share with the Teutonic Knights another crusade against these Saracens of the north. On his way he had given chivalric dances and fêtes in honor of women in Breslau and Thorn and other German cities and had been himself sumptuously welcomed by the Grand Master at Königsberg. No court in Europe was set against a background of greater splendor than that of these knights who had developed worldly ambition and were a formidable secular power, controlling large Baltic territories and many cities.

The world, people believed, could not match their Marienburg fortress on the banks of the Nogat which branched off from the great Vistula at its Baltic delta. To those sailing in barges down the river, the Order's church and palace towers and gigantic walls lifting one above the other were visible from a great distance. The more eastern Königsberg seat was less imposing though it had great strategic importance. It was from there that Duke Albert and his hosts, with united forces, had advanced into Lithuania, to burn and punish on infidel soil. During eight days they harried the land of Olgierd and his eleven warrior sons, amongst whom they most feared the seventh, Jagiello, a believer in amulets and in his predestined luck in war.

As the child-lovers sat shiveringly following Suchenwirt's recital, was there some strange premonitory sense that chilled the eagerness with which little Jadwiga's betrothed, half-married Prince of the Habsburgs listened while the chevalier poet described?

Then came vital news for Jadwiga. Her parents had called her home. Her heart leaped! Yet she knew that William's father had not consented to her going. Despite the kindness with which she was surrounded, how hard it had been to be away from Mary and her mother and father. She would not forget friendly, peace-loving Duke Albert and the things he had taught her, but she wanted to go home. Nor had it been easy for her parents to have her away. Neither King Louis nor Queen Elizabeth dared face the personal grief or the dynastic danger that the loss of either remaining daughter would bring. They wanted to feel both beside them.

The queen mother, Elizabeth, having fled from trouble in Poland, was in Hungary. Jadwiga longed to see her grandmother, to whom Louis' children were as dear to her as her own, which was saying much. Her right hand bore mute and terrible witness to her maternal love and courage—only one finger remained. People were careful not to talk much or too openly about this mutilation, for the story behind it was no credit to a civilized court. During Charles

Robert's reign, because of a wrong done to beautiful Clara Zach, a maid of honor, by King Casimir who was visiting at Visegrád, Clara's infuriated father had rushed in upon the royal family as they sat in the dining-hall, and thrust right and left with his sword. When he attacked Louis and his brother Andrew, their mother had leaped in front of them and with uplifted hand stopped the sword. Her treasurer, rushing to the rescue, had felled the father with a bronze pole axe, and others had finished him off. The rest of the story the court preferred to forget; for the punishment visited on the unfortunate Clara and her brothers and sisters belonged to savage rather than Christian annals.

At this time the devoted mother was discussing again with her son the Polish succession prospects. He welcomed her counsel. It was she who had helped him to win the first consent of the Poles to his proposal that one of his daughters should inherit their crown—for in Poland, as in Hungary, the magnates maintained their right to choose from the reigning line, the new king. It seemed wise to call a meeting of the Poles at once to reaffirm their promises. But winter, and spring with its melting snows, were bad times for congresses, so mother and son decided to let matters run along until summer.

Then it was that the king further pressed Duke Leopold to shorten the time of Jadwiga's stay in Austria and send her home to Hungary. At first the Habsburg had refused to consider this change of plan; he, too, was looking to the security of this alliance, and it seemed safer with William's fiancée at his own court. However, he decided to discuss this and other matters personally with Louis, and after his journey to Buda, it was arranged that Jadwiga should return. And William, with her, was to continue his training in Hungary. He must be not only perfectly familiar with the duties of knighthood, but with Magyar customs; he must understand the achievements and the ambitions of the country over which he would one day rule.

What joy for Jadwiga! She was to regain her family, and without losing her friend. In her thoughts, William was already an inseparable part of that family. The journey eastward, with their pet dogs and horses, past the Cathedral-crowned hill of Hainburg so indelibly engraved on their fresh minds, along the broad river, between the bright hill lands they loved, was a continuously exciting experience. Did elders, watching, find poignant as well as amusing, the swift shifts between romping boy and girl and grave and gallant knight and his princess lady-love? During these days the jubilant girl was uppermost. She was going home—going to Mary and her mother and father, to Visegrád, where the Danube would curve around the hill base. That meant leapings and snatches of song, rosy cheeks and loosened tresses.

At Visegrád, on the palace terrace on the narrow river plain, there was a tumult of welcoming as Jadwiga was gathered into royal arms. Queen Elizabeth did not try to conceal glad tears. King Louis, wearing this day the surcoat of the Anjevin family—azure, sown with golden fleur de lys, lifted her high. And after the embraces and happy questionings of the elders, she and William were crowned with rose and lilac wreaths by the younger group, and escorted with singing and noisy joyance to the Salamon tower-palace on the steep hillside.

Several palaces lifted from this royal hill. There was room in them for the entertainment of two kings and many minor princes with all their suites. "Eagles' Nest" restless rulers had called Visegrád, "from whose rocky summit we can watch and at whose water-lapped base we can enjoy." And they encircled it with granite walls and towers. On the outcropping rock of the crest they raised a stern combination of fortress—chateau and church, whose forbidding upper level could be reached by ladder only. Two-thirds down the steep slope they set the more accessible Salamon tower palace where King Louis and his family usually lived. And on the sandy plain between the Danube beach and the hill rise, ran a girdle of palaces, furnished with great splendor and surrounded by gardens of rarest flowers. Here days of festival and tournament unfolded; often at night music from the higher towers floated down upon the scene. It was not surprising that the young people of the court, as well as their elders, preferred Eagles' Nest to any other place they knew.

In Salamon Tower Jadwiga was escorted past the

lower kitchens and dining rooms up to the fourth of the six floors. This was the women's floor. Below it were the king's quarters and above it the knights'. It was divided into four chambers, of which Queen Elizabeth's with its great fire-place, yellow plastered walls hung with brilliant tapestries, and tiled limestone floor made comfortable by fur and eastern rugs, was the most important. The children loved its deeply recessed windows giving from alcoved platforms which they reached by wooden steps. From one window they looked on the emerald hill slope and breathed pine and fir fragrances; from the opposite one they peered dizzyingly down on the Danube. This room was Jadwiga's home at Visegrad.

Not long after her return her father summoned the Polish magnates to a meeting to reconsider the disposition of the Polish crown. King Louis called them in August, 1379, to the northern walled city of Kassa, where Hungary's most beautiful gothic Cathedral stood, and where he had built, too, a palace to facilitate just such conferences. To this pleasant city the arbiters of Poland's future came, but by no means single-mindedly. The powerful Polish archbishop of Gnezno, Bodzanta, who ranked next to the king, and the nobles of Great Poland, strongly opposed Louis' plan to make his eldest daughter, Mary, their queen. While Dobieslaw, castellan of Capital Hill at Krakow, and the nobles of the province of Small Poland in which Krakow lay, even more strongly supported it. This conflict the swift and vigorous Louis handled in his characteristic manner. He shut the gates at Kassa, and declared that nobody would leave until the opposition was beaten. Thus coerced, the Poles obediently declared that Mary would be their future queen!

And a few months later, at a meeting in the hunting castle at Zólym, Louis and the two Elizabeths and Leopold agreed that the marriage of William and Jadwiga would take place just as soon as William was twelve years old.

CHAPTER III

Happy Days on Eagles' Nest

High up on Visegrád Hill between an oak and pine covered slope and the next rise toward the east, is a meadow. It is a snow-drop and violet garden in spring, and later in the year, is aflame with fireweed and asters and wild roses. Because of its wet soil all flowers bloom there longer than in most other places.

On this autumn midday, Mary and her fiancé, Prince Sigismund, and William and Jadwiga, and a half dozen others excused early from lessons, had climbed up to the starry field with poles and nets. Peter, whose father before him had been one of the royal chefs, had offered to prepare for their dinner any fish they might catch. All week they had been making farewell tours to favorite spots, for the court was soon to move down to Buda for the winter. They were, in fact, fishing en route to a higher objective, the fortress on the summit, where always interesting buildings and restoring were going on, and where King Louis had promised this day to make an inspection.

The royal family had not lived in the uppermost castle for some time, and to encourage the soldiers and others who must remain on the crest while court life centered 750 feet below, the king had arranged to have dinner there *al fresco.* He was passionately devoted to outdoor festivities, above all to the chase—no one could please him better than by accompanying him on a hunt. But because in the busy week preceding the transfer of the court down the river, hunting was not to be thought of, he now particularly welcomed a picnic. Fortunately, in their pleasure in out-of-doors the king and queen found their tastes, as in other things, congenial. Elizabeth loved gaiety and informality, and delighted in every opportunity for an excursion with her husband or her children. Before starting on the hill climb, King Louis was saying farewell to envoys from Venice come on the important business of an extension of the Hungarian-Venetian truce.

The daughter of the Governor of Ruthenia, Elizabeth, was leader of the young people's advance ascent. She was between Jadwiga and Mary in age, dark-haired, dark-eyed, warm-hearted, and a favorite with them all, as she was with the queen herself, to whom she had been sent to be educated. She had been named after Queen Elizabeth and Jadwiga's grandmother—another Elizabeth; one threaded one's way through Elizabeths and Johns!

There was an especial bond between this Elizabeth and Jadwiga, which was to strengthen with the years. Today they made a charming picture, both in straight falling, girdled dresses of green silk. Mary, too, was in green, a favorite color for outdoor wear. She was quieter than the others, and was twisting wreaths of wild roses for them, while Jadwiga and Elizabeth, off on the hillside beside a waterfall, were stooping and sliding as they gathered fronds in which to wrap the carp William and Sigismund had caught.

These princes, clad in comfortable short brown coats, and close-fitting, bright-hued under garments, were still casting their nets. They were good comrades despite sharp differences in disposition and character, and despite the fact that Sigismund, who was several years older than William, did not conceal his feeling of superiority. Both were German; they were destined to be royal brothers-in-law. William admired Sigismund's greater vigor and was usually ready to forgive his ruder ways. Often others were not and it was well known that the queen found him unsympathetic.

On the meadow everyone was happy. There was a shout over each silvery addition to the pile on the bank ready for wrapping, and another shout when an adventurer sank into the oozing sand. A wreath finished, Mary called Jadwiga from the waterfall and set it crownwise upon her shining hair—she should always be thus flower-crowned. Mary adored her younger sister. No one was so proud as she when at the annual voting, the pages and girls of the court had chosen "Jadza" as beauty queen, Queen of Pentecost. She did seem literally to grow lovelier each month, her cheeks rosier, her blue eyes darker, her hair more luxuriantly sunny. There was no difference of opinion as to which flower she represented; her glowing beauty and her intensity made her always the rose. They lived in intimate companionship, these children, with flowers and trees and animals, each having for them its vivid individual personality.

Here on the meadow the fishing was often interrupted by a game of chase, of improvised flower-question and response—to sing and dance were as natural and essential as to breathe and eat.

"Are you a rose or are you a tulip?"—John caught the fleeing Elizabeth.

> "I am a rose, but beware, I have thorns,
> No tulip has a heart so proud as mine."

The evening before, at the farewell dance, where pages had carried bright-colored silk pillows, girls had worn wreaths of favorite flowers. That concluding function was the absorbing subject of conversation on the way to the hilltop. How many times the coquette, Dorothy, had turned aside as Toldi glided toward her, ready to drop his pillow and kneel at her feet, and thus accepted, kiss and whirl her away! He had had to dance past, while she sang teasingly after him:

> "The student sits with a book.
> And reads about love from a book;
> The page does not sit,
> He loves a hundred girls without a recipe.
> Why should I look at either?"

The sun had crossed the zenith, and the castle was a good half hour above. Elizabeth gave the order to proceed. They must reach the top long enough ahead of the royal suite to have plenty of time with Peter in the kitchen.

Jadwiga ran to William with her ferns. They wrapped their fish and with the others began climbing. Often the pages pushed forward, running across a damp, mossy slope under conifers and oaks to recover the narrow, zigzagging road above. Their loosely pointed shoes made of soft skin and bound about the ankles with thongs, though insufficient protection against sharp stones, made running over soft banks almost as pleasant as if one were barefoot.

Each was eager to round the corner which gave the first full view of the fortress. How powerfully the two concentric walls encircled the hilltop, and how splendidly the church tower lifted from within. How blue the sky against which the gray pile stood—how darkly blue the ridges sweeping far to the north and far to the south on either side of the winding bronze river below. No wonder people came from the corners of Europe to see Eagles' Nest, and that wandering minstrels never tired of describing it.

When at last the straggling company, more or less breathlessly, reached the moat, the drawbridge had already been lowered by its heavy chains and the oak portcullis raised. The guards who usually sat on the stone benches at either side of the deep-walled gate, and those from the oak balcony encircling it above, came joyously to meet them, and after the ceremonial greeting, lifting the younger ones to their shoulders, with singing and questioning escorted them within. They swung first around the great western wall, then following the second, passed through another gateway into the long, narrow courtyard. From there they saw on his threshold at the farther end, white-haired Chef Peter waving a frantic welcome with a kitchen towel.

They ran tumultuously toward him, past the king's quarters on the left and the queen's on the right, straight to his smoky, sizzling domain. Such welcoming!—and the warmest, as ever, for Jadwiga and William. Beneath their youthfulness and joyous carefreeness were a thoughtfulness and modesty that endeared them to all their elders.

There was much running to and fro inside the kitchen through whose duskiness shot the flames of open fires. It seemed more populated than a small fair. One servant, a fat capon in hand, was watching a kettle over a corner chimney fire—"Until the water can no longer remain in its own skin," he said. And then, plump, he submerged it, and after leaving it just long enough, lifted it quickly, to wipe away feathers and nails. Another was skinning a lamb, a third greasing a thin hare, while over farther coals, one turned a little pig on a spit, and with the reverse edge of a knife scraped off its hair. The fact that the great poet Petrarch, a vegetarian, had expressed his disgust of "yellow and black lumps of flesh" served at a noon day meal," had no whit discouraged the meat-eating Hungarians! Cheeses lay in rows on long boards; the white and dark bread loaves were already molded; someone was hanging up a goatskin full of wine; others were taking down lambskins of flour and beating dozens of eggs and great bowls of cream for puddings. The visitors were everywhere at once, tasting here, whiffing there in an ecstasy of inspection, while Peter himself, now lordly in manner, was patting and rolling and otherwise impressively preparing their own fish.

There was so much to do, so much to see, that it seemed no time at all before the silver trumpets announced the arrival of the king and queen at the great gate. Now it was the young people's turn to welcome, and tearing themselves away from the crackling delights, they raced down the courtyard to the gate.

Louis' informal outdoor costume, a soft, brown skin coat over his green tunic and tight green hose, subtracted nothing from his majestic appearance. Assurance, valor, an optimistic and generous outlook, spoke from both countenance and bearing. He was at all times meticulously careful about his clothes and expected others to be; rarely did a knight dare to approach him with a soiled cassock beneath his coat of mail. The young people knew that he would romp with them later, but now they deeply saluted their king. In this costume he resembled the Louis who often travelled incognito over the land, arriving unexpectedly to ask for a night's lodging of some member of the gentry or peasantry, in the hope that in friendly conversation, he might discover what the people truly thought of his rule.

This genuine interest in his subjects' welfare and their resulting confidence in him, had made it possible for Louis to rule practically as absolute monarch, even though Hungary had its Magna Charta and Louis had on his accession been made to swear to uphold it and to call the stipulated diets. As a matter of fact he assembled them rarely; for he preferred to transact the real business of state through his royal council, where, however, he gave confidential positions, not only to traditional arbiters, but to members of the class below them—to capable representatives of the lower nobility, to influential burghers, and often to Italians. In thus choosing persons for important posts from hitherto untried ranks, the independent Louis was creating a new Hungarian aristocracy.

He was riding forth less frequently now, either in quest of reactions to his rule, or on the hunt; for despite his outward appearance of vigor, his inner vitality had been sapped by the too strenuous years. He worked hard until midday but in the afternoon he needed diversion and such a simple festivity as this was measured to his strength. Today he had climbed the hill with as much zest as had Elizabeth, whose woodsy costume of russet and green and coif of fine lawn turned back from her forehead, were especially becoming. She and her women carried baskets of woven willow withes in which they had been gathering ferns and roots to take to Buda for replanting.

Seeing the king and queen thus together, one understood Elizabeth's influence with Louis, and why, neither patriots nor intriguers had been able to turn one against the other.

All went first to the church, and after prayers, the queen, with Mary and Jadwiga and Elizabeth and the other young girls, mounted the stairway leading from the nave to her rooms built into it as a kind of second story. At the same time the court ladies went outside and up to a higher cliff level to their apartments, from which they could pass directly to the queen's rooms.

There they washed in silver basins and freshened their toilets, while the king's suite did likewise at the opposite side of the courtyard. They may not have used tubs often, but they were continually washing. Even for this brief outing the ladies had brought along quantities of their favorite perfume, Reine d'Hongrie. The queen mother herself had devised the recipe—what didn't that astonishing, bright-eyed, fresh-complexioned, old lady know? It was supposed to possess magical power to preserve youth, and they were certain that it helped to cure rheumatism.

Meanwhile, the long tables were being spread, musicians were setting the small portable organ in place and getting ready their flutes and zithers. Jadwiga's white sheep dog and other privileged hounds were running about in confident anticipation. The princesses themselves decorated with asters and sunflowers the table already heaped with nuts and bright apples and golden grapes. Queen Elizabeth would be at the head of the royal table; for she always had the place of honor and was served first.

Chef Peter had outdone himself. He felt that his dishes were particularly well spiced; the royal family, like all Hungarians, enjoyed highly seasoned food. And his wines had been properly chilled in the ice caves; for cold drinks went well with high seasoning. When, after all had found their places, he advanced with exaggerated pace to the accompaniment of a spirited march, holding high a great silver platter bearing a boar's head with an apple in its mouth and surrounded by elks' nostrils and by bears' feet, and deposited it with a magnificent flourish before the laughing Louis, there was general hand-clapping and shouting.

The young people had never seen the king in happier mood. He engaged in lively exchanges with the young heir of Naples, Charles of Durazzo, whom he had attached almost as a member of his family. Even the court astrologer Matthias, whom he usually treated with much seriousness, was the victim of his wit. Between courses he called the betrothed couples to him, teasing and admonishing them, to the delight of the others, until they were rescued by the laughing Elizabeth. To an appeal for a story he responded with a hair-raising narrative of an encounter with pagan bandits, and then himself called for a song and led them with clapping and stamping.

How many courses? How many amusing tales told,

what cracks by the jester and swift rejoinders? How many happy after dinner adventures under the blue sky? Their climax was the climb up the ladder to the innermost stronghold—even the king could reach it only by the ladder stairway. From there the whole world of danger and beauty lay unrolled below. On the leisurely way homeward, and many a time afterward, Jadwiga and William talked over together particularly remembered pleasures of this day.

One compensation for having to leave Visegrád, was the journey on barges to Buda some thirty miles down stream. There was always a long procession of these barges bearing the king and queen, their suites, dogs and other animals, and furnishings—everything could be piled easily on the long, broad-bottomed boats that floated on the current. They needed only the occasional pull of one of the long ropes attached to the accompanying horses on shore, and other occasional guiding by the long oars. There was no question as to the way the young people of the court preferred to travel. The excitements of navigating a river procession far exceeded those of the progress of a cavalcade. These lasted from the initial thrill of being taken in canoes to the main barge floating the red and white flags of the Magyars, and being pulled up over its side, to the very end of the journey.

Clustered on every available free space on this barge, were farewell gifts. Shepherds had brought their finest cheeses, vineyardists from the sunny slopes opposite Visegrád, great baskets of purple grapes and skins of golden wine of old vintage. There were other baskets of pears and little prunes of Saint Catherine, and off in a corner was a low tub of fresh water lobsters. As they started, they could hear the dogs barking in Maros across the river, where they often went to swim.

All day long the barge bearing the Anjevin family floated beside the willow and poplar fringed bank from which innumerable white geese noisily protested their presence. They wound around small low-clustered villages with thatched roofs and larger ones with slate roofs—all of them bright with autumn gardens and bowery with linden trees. Long wagons, drawn by long-horned oxen, and piled high with lumber or kegs or baskets of fruit and vegetables, plied between these hamlets. Farther to the right of the broad river course ran the splendid Saint Pilis Mountain ranges, oak forested, and rich in minerals, and below them fields of wheat and rye. Hills topped by castle or monastery passed in unending panorama. While again and again from the plain or the near roadside, some fragment of palace, or of the Roman wall and aqueduct that once paralleled the Danube, thrust into view.

There were innumerable reminders of the great Roman days and of the city of Acquincum which flourished in the second century. The road beyond the river beach had been a kind of Appian Way flanked by tombs and palaces and baths. Now the spires and bell towers of Christian cloisters and chapels looked down on what time and the Turks had left of the

Roman structures. Jadwiga and Mary always watched especially for the ruins of the Coliseum, which they often visited; it had been almost as large as that in Rome.

On reaching the low-lying town of Old Buda, still one of the royal headquarters, they were about a half hour from their objective, Buda Hill, destined to become the single national capital. The point between Old Buda and the Hill, on which their young attention chiefly centered, was lovely Saint Margaret's Island. Here, too, there had been Roman palaces and baths and temples but what interested them chiefly, was the romantic story of Saint Margaret, whose name the island now bore. A visit to its convent was one of Queen Elizabeth's favorite outings.

For Jadwiga and William this was history learned not out of musty books or by dry preachments but rather actually lived as they floated silently by castle and hill and chapel, listening to legends repeated by court teachers and singers in whose tales and songs yesterday and today seemed indistinguishable.

CHAPTER IV

The Court at Buda

Now it was on high bastioned Buda Hill that forces seen and unseen were forging the fate of Jadwiga and William. As they went back and forth between palace and church, on their walks around the rim of the hill, or followed their program of study and play, those who watched, instead of saying, "There go the happy comrades," were more apt to say, "There go Hungary's queen and king."

The picture of life here, as at Visegrád, was the continually changing mirror of feudal times. The days presented amazing contrasts as the exquisite forms of the Renaissance flowered to the accompaniment of clashing steel. King Louis gathered about him a complete hierarchy of nobles, many of whom he richly endowed. And about them, in turn, were grouped, in banderia, the military forces of the kingdom, each with its own pennant. No others surpassed them in dash and splendor as they assembled on important occasions.

This was a time of territorial fluidity, with national crystallization still in the future. Dynastic states were but beginning to shape themselves, and because of yet unharnessed, powerful nobles, their kings were often scarcely masters in their own house. On the turbulent European scene fell continually the shadow of the two empires; of the eastern one, centered in Constantinople and drawing life from the orthodox church, and the western one, leaning on Rome and the Papacy. Hungary held a peculiar position of balance between these two empires, which meant a constant challenge to her diplomatic skill.

Louis was proud of the bond between himself and his army, whose swiftness and daring astonished other troops. An admiring Italian observer described them as relying confidently on the accuracy of their arrows' aim in offense and on the skill with which they handled the long sword in defense. "Their horses," he said, "are accustomed to rain as are their knights, whose long saddles serve as outdoor beds. . . . They do not suffer from hunger in desert regions for they carry in their bags a dry meat powder which, thrown into boiling water, suffices them. They excel in swiftness, in flight, shoot their arrows, and, turning abruptly, recommence the battle. . . . They seek the greatest peril, disregarding death."

Nor did the great Louis neglect his navy. His interest in his sailors was not less than that in his soldiers; he considered his Magyar boatmen second only to the Venetians in dexterity and surety. He demanded for his outpost country assured access to the sea; for a country to have access to the sea was to be able to breathe. The Magyars must connect with the magical seas and with the ever-growing world of wonder and opportunity being uncovered by the followers of Marco Polo. Louis' ships carrying grain and minerals from the Hungarian plains and mountains to Dalmatia and there exchanging their cargoes for stuffs and spices and perfumes arrived from Asia, must be protected along their routes. In this naval effort, the Danube was his chief asset. He indefatigably built for it a supporting system of roads and bridges. These he protected against robbers, while he walled in his mill towns, and gave others greater safety.

In the Neapolitan campaigns, during which they had thus impressed the Italians, the Hungarian nobility had been in turn deeply impressed by Italian art and culture, whose influence was soon expressed in the domestic architecture and in the gardens and fresco painting and sculpture of their own country. This development Louis encouraged. He was ambitious to keep his capital abreast of Paris and the beauty-loving cities of Europe, especially of the luminous metropolis, nearby Prague. Therefore he called artists and workmen to Buda not only from the ecstatic workshops of Italy, but from those of France and Germany and farther-away places until out of a combination of Magyar richness of color and design with more delicate western forms he achieved a background of varied beauty. In addition to the royal arms of Hungary, the crowned eagle and plumes, one saw everywhere the graceful Anjevin device, the lily of France. It blossomed on scepter and crown and mantle, above gateways and doorways, and on the cloths and rugs that gave warmth and softness to rugged halls. The palace shone with a wealth of gem-studded crosses and images, crystal bowls and gold cups, ivory toilet articles, silver table services. There were, too, linens of finest weave and handsomely carved furniture—tables stood ready for games of dice and draughts.

The custom of lavish gift-giving greatly stimulated artistic endeavor. Rarely was there an important occasion which omitted the presentation of handsome cups or other souvenirs. And King Louis gave not only within his own borders but to far-away courts and churches. The chapel he built at Aachen in memory of a victory over the Turks, treasured from him three madonnas in silver frames carved with the Polish eagle, several gilded candlesticks and six pieces of beautiful armor.

Despite the richness of interiors, at Buda, as at Visegrád, guests were often welcomed out-of-doors. When, for instance, the year after the "False Marriage," the Scalas of Italy arrived for a visit, King Louis received them under a blue velvet tent, embroidered in gold and glittering with amethysts and pearls. Chairs inside the tent were inlaid with ivory and gold figures of animals and flowers. Above it were tree branches and birds, and the guests themselves were crowned with leaves as they entered. Even Italy with its Doge's Palace, Lily Tower, and blossoming of beauty that stirred the world, could scarcely have enhanced the picture. Was it surprising, then, that artists and poets and the celebrated scholars whom Louis encouraged to come to Buda, found it a sympathetic capital?

This ardent son of the Church ever welcomed, too, priest and friar—chapel services were in progress almost continuously. He himself, people said, did between two and three hundred Aves daily. And Mary and Jadwiga began early to emulate their father's example. Across Europe fourteenth century faith flowered in marvelous spires. They lifted from chapel and cloister—music of religion—pointing from the uncertainty of terrestrial possessions to the certainty of celestial treasure. However long the arm of the Turk or of the black plague (twice pestilence had all but wiped out Louis' people) it could not reach the kingdom of heaven. Angels easily negotiated the airways between that heaven and earth. King Louis envied those who could live entirely in this mystical world. How soon would he be able to let the burdens of kingship slip to the shoulders of his sons-in-law that he might end his days in contemplation? He liked to ask this question—whose answer was always postponed!

On the continent there was a continual exchange of teachers and students. This was augmented by the custom, in certain important schools—most schools were under control of the religious Orders—of awarding scholarships instead of degrees. Thus, some of Hungary's schools gave scholarships for the University of Paris. One found Hungarian students, too, at Oxford and Cologne, at Vienna and Padua. Among others whom the king brought to the second Hungarian University, which he founded at Pécs, and whose progress he followed with keen interest, was the famous law professor, Bettini, of Bologna, whom he treated with great munificence. The young people heard much of this university, especially Jadwiga and William, who would one day be responsible for its development.

The arrival of a scholar or singer was always an exciting event to the betrothed comrades. They had a natural vivid curiosity about the world beyond Hungary and Austria. They plied such visitors with questions, begging especially for news of battles in France where the Hundred Years War was dragging on its weary length and where no one yet saw on the horizon the Maid of Orleans, soon to appear. They were ever eager, too, for reports of how things were going with young King Richard of England, not much older than they, and for recitals of the fascinating tales of his poet Chaucer—they wished this tale-teller might be induced to come himself to Buda.

They gleaned much from scribes and painters and other artists. They were especially at home in Scribe John of Aprod's study, where the chronicle of the reign was being written. Jadwiga's father encouraged these visits; he himself followed with much satisfaction the writing of this record and the other bookmaking at his court; one reason why the silent Carthusian monks enjoyed his marked favor was because of the beauty of their manuscripts. He prized his own books far beyond gold and silver cups, and most, perhaps, his beautifully printed edition of the Moral Reflections of Pope Gregory on Job, made for him in Visegrád by John Bredensheid; then a psalter in three languages—Latin, German, and Polish, and a particularly exquisite missal.

William and Jadwiga spent hours together in Scribe John's study looking over the historian's shoulder. While he worked, he told them of the marvelous Madonnas, all a glory of gold and deep blues and reds, being painted at the court of Emperor John Paleologos at Constantinople, and described workshops in Greece and elsewhere. Brimming with curiosity, they examined the little metal and earthenware pots of powders and the brushes and knives and other magical bookshop properties. And when Scribe John, seating them before a table and a sheet of parchment, helped them to encircle their initials with birds and budding vines, they were enchanted.

They were welcome visitors, too, in the studios of the famous sculptor brothers, Martin and George, sons of the painter Nicholas of Kolosvari. There they were allowed to model with clay while admiring the wonderful statues of Saint George and Saint Stephen that grew under these artists' fingers. Sometimes their older friend Bishop Valentine of Pécs, or Knight Toldi, another friend, accompanied them on such visits.

Then there were the fascinating silversmith's workrooms—and in all of these places, what a joyous atmosphere! Everywhere men were working for the sheer love of creating; usually they did not sign their masterpieces, saying rather, "We do not want our names, but our works, to be written in the Book of Life."

Louis paid particular attention to the beauty of his coins. When the state had claimed the gold and silver of the mines, those precious metals had been hidden from collectors. But after the Anjevins wisely reduced their claims to but one-third of the output, the mines flourished, and there was enough gold to furnish coins as beautiful as the Florentine ducat—these had the fleur de lys on one face and an image of John the Baptist on the other. One of the most admired coins represented the king kneeling before the Blessed Virgin.

No city in Europe offered a more stimulating natural setting for such creative activity. Paris on the Seine, London on the Thames, Florence on the Arno, Venice on the Adriatic, all had especial claims to beauty of position; but no other capital possessed Buda's dramatic conjunction of hills, river, and plain. Less intimate and exquisite than Visegrád, it had a compensating grandeur. The Hungarians, after choosing first the lower site of old Buda, had later selected these heights whose defensive walls and bastions now lifted mightily from the Danube. Secret stairways within these walls dropped to the river below, and water from the reservoir into which the river water was strained, was carried up to the palace along them. On the same hill from which embassies today look on an incomparable panorama, these fourteenth century fortifications commanded the mountain hinterland and the river and plain foreground. Across the stream, facing Buda, and connected with it by a bridge of boats, lay Pest. Often in the evening one ran to the ramparts to watch the lowering light gilding its church towers and low roofs.

In the morning there were usually silvery mists and soft puffs of cloud above the magical water, sweeping, curving, with the hills. And at certain times of the year billowy fog quite concealed it. The chateau awakened to the sounds of the rasping and creaking of lifting bridge and portcullis, the clanking of metal and polishing of armor. Then the cackling of geese and crowing of cocks, the barking of dogs and neighing of horses, heralded the change of guards. Halloos of boatmen drifted up from canoes and barges and from the road the cries of cows and sheep and goats, or the songs of pilgrim processions already under way. A part of the world was ever on foot or on horse, called by a shrine, a war, a crusade, a discovery of truth—life offered one joyous incentive after another to wandering.

Thus was placed this Magyar court, Jadwiga's home, where she was being taught to be a queen. And here King Louis himself was the chief instructor of Mary and Jadwiga, and during their sojourn at Visegrád and Buda, of Sigismund and William also. No other princesses in Europe were being educated as were these two girls, although because nature had more liberally endowed Jadwiga, she profited most. Louis not only supervised what others taught them, but step by step, as they grew ready, unfolded to their fresh minds his conceptions and his hopes for the Magyar realm. He was qualified to teach; for he possessed not only a thorough theoretical knowledge of the science of government as it was then understood, but in his successful application of that knowledge had established himself as one of the great executives of the western world.

This court was one of Europe's best training schools—it was in fact a kind of educational institution for children of the nobility. Lower only than his ideal of religious zeal and piety, King Louis set his standard of hardness and endurance in word and deed. Each great noble hoped for his son the good fortune to receive at least part of his preparation for knighthood under the great king, a preparation which began at an age when our children are still in their nurseries. The younger pages in their silks and velvets were the joy of the palace. They could scarcely begin too early to learn religion, dancing, singing, and the elements of good manners. They must not put their fingers in the mustard-pot or other general dishes, but use instead a fresh crust of bread or a spoon; there must be no blowing on food to cool it, no elbow on the table, no using of the tablecloth as towel, or picking of teeth with knives!

In the fencing contests the best page got a green cap, just as the best knight received a crown of laurel or of roses from the most beautiful lady. Every page aspired to become that victorious knight, and under the general patronage of Saint George and the especial patronage of Saint Ladislaus of Hungary, to succor the distressed and serve God and the earthly King, who would reward him with gold and silver gifts and horses and armor. If lucky, he might attain the order of Saint George or the Golden Spur. Similarly, every girl longed one day to be the awarding Queen of Beauty. Very recently she had been chosen from no less than two hundred ladies all dressed in green velvet trimmed with gold and ermine, who had assembled to witness a tournament in honor of Venus. William would one day wear Jadwiga's scarf on his arm, and from her hands receive the crown!

The royal children were, of course, taught earlier than others. Among their many instructors, both of the laity and the clergy, none was more influential than the Bishop of Veszprem, Ladislaus Demendi. One of the best educated men at court, an intimate friend of the family, and Queen Elizabeth's chancellor, he was at the same time her physician. He had, in fact, brought Jadwiga into the world, and for that successful delivery had been rewarded with a fine palace in Upper Hungary.

The country had ardently hoped that this third child would be the long looked-for male heir. At times powerful nobles had gone so far as to suggest that the king put away Elizabeth and take a wife on whom he might rely for sons. The queen mother herself once urged this course on her son, who reluctantly agreed to follow it. And Elizabeth in the generosity of her great love, had consented to a separation. She and Louis went sadly to Dalmatia together, to establish there, at Zara, a monastery, before they parted. But as the severing weeks passed, they knew themselves more deeply in love than ever before, and when the queen found that she was again pregnant, they retracted their promises, and returned joyfully to Buda!

Once, before a child was to be born, King Louis had made the long journey with his wife to Ragusa, there to pray before the holy relics of Saint Simeon for a male heir, but, as it proved, again without avail. It was at this time that rumor reported that the queen had stolen a finger bone of the Saint, to help her to the hoped-for delivery, but after a series of punitive illnesses had returned it! Whether she purloined the sacred finger or not, she did order made in Ragusa a more suitable casket in which to enshrine Saint Simeon's body—a splendid silver ark, set with portrait placques of the king and queen and their suites, which it took four years to complete. Everyone at court followed reports of its progress.

The Bishop of Veszprem often recounted to Jadwiga the story of these disappointed hopes, adding that God would once again demonstrate his inscrutable wisdom, when, through her rule with William, the Hungarian people would win hitherto unknown glory and well-being.

Scribe John, was another favorite teacher. History lessons never lagged, and especially for Mary. Referring to her enthusiasm, John, in dedicating a book to her, wrote, "One of the signs of an immortal soul is that it can see beyond its own boundaries." Besides history and geography lessons, and the scholastic grammar and rhetoric, there were languages to be learned. To begin with, educated persons must know the international language, Latin. Zealous Christians aspired further; they wished to read the psalms and other portions of the scriptures in the original Hebrew. And to the future queens, Mary and Jadwiga, and to William and Sigismund, after Hungarian, German and Polish were of first importance, with Italian and French following close upon them. With a knowledge of French and Italian, what treasure of lyric and epic and romantic literature lay before one! Deprived indeed were those who had not read at least the choicest love songs of the troubadours, the knightly Arthurian romances, the writings of Saint Francis, Dante's Divine Comedy and Petrarch's sonnets. Polish was more difficult than these Latin tongues. King Louis himself had never taken the trouble to master the Poles' language, which did not lessen his difficulties as absentee king of their country.

As they grew older, Jadwiga's and Mary's lessons included more than this program. The king greatly honored in women simplicity in manners and appearance, and proficiency in the arts and in all that pertained to the management of the household. So that unusually early Queen Elizabeth began their instruction in the simpler duties of the ménage. She was expert in embroidery and her daughters loved to sit beside her, drawing their own designs, matching seed pearls and coral, and silk and metal threads. No visitor could please them more than by bringing them gifts of coveted embroidery materials. Their mother superintended, too, their music lessons, occasionally supplementing them with exercises of her own invention. Those were wonderful hours, when as a reward for a task well performed, accompanying herself on the lute, she sang to them, songs wild as the mountains and soft as the valleys of Bosnia. Sometimes she sang lilting tunes of her own Polish mother's country—she liked thinking of herself as half Polish.

But aside from this intimate instruction, the queen exercised far less complete control over the education of her daughters than she might have had, had she possessed the influence of her mother-in-law with the king, or had she been endowed with the gifts and character of that old lady.

Sometimes, it is true, the queen mother was criticized as too pleasure-loving and temperamental to be intrusted with her responsibilities. But those who rightly measured her powers said that she was more like a man than a woman in her independence and open-mindedness. They knew her to be the first woman in Hungary to have so large an influence in political and social affairs. Vivid and individual, she had been independent even of the Pope in politics—a fact which did not encourage the papal chroniclers to overestimate her abilities! Her court at Krakow was indeed one of the gayest in Europe—the queen regent at seventy-five still led the dance, but while she was listening to poets and singers, her cities, despite internal disorders, were thriving, and Poland's industry and trade were growing. That was her answer to critics. One chronicler in summing up her qualities said of her that "she loved lusty gaiety, founded churches and convents and read her breviary hard." It was just this combination of *joie de vivre* and religious fervor that made her so wonderful to her grandchildren.

CHAPTER V.

Growing Up

This preparation of a girl to be queen and a boy to be king was no light matter. If anybody imagined the future rulers of Hungary and Poland as idling through the years of their minority, he was far from the truth. Yet there were many holy days and festivals to break the routine of study.

At times, too, work was turned to play, as when one day Knight Stephen, William's instructor in the use of the lance, staged a mimic match between himself and his pupil. Elders were quick to fall in with the happy idea. Nicholas of Gara, Chief Justice Jacob, Doctors Radlica and Demendi, Szechenyi, and other officers of the court and visiting knights gathered with dames and ladies in waiting and a large group of young people in the courtyard on the crest of Buda Hill, just as they would have assembled to witness a serious tourney.

They made a brilliant splash of color against the palace walls—the women in close-fitting silk and velvet robes, with flowing veils and fluted head-dresses and elaborate hats; the men, as well, gay in bright tunics and hats and hose and pointed shoes of contrasting hues. It would have been difficult to say which gleamed more splendidly, the feminine gold and ivory combs and circlets or the masculine belts and scabbards. With the company was a visiting French knight whose dark curls were caught in a jewelled net. He had a gladsome expression in his eye and was frankly proud of the short damascened travelling sword which the group around him were examining. It was engraved with the motto, "With this good sword and God's will I will still the cries of mine enemies."

For a moment talk ceased as the dark-eyed queen, in an embroidered dress and fur-edged mantle, with the two princesses, joined the company. Then it resumed in accelerated tempo. And quickly Knight Stephen led his youthful opponent to the middle of the jousting place.

William, though much taller than when he stood before the altar with Jadwiga at Hainburg, still looked frail. Today he wore a red tunic embroidered with the Habsburg eagle, and as always gave an impression of elegance. He was exceedingly graceful and his blue eyes were bright with excitement over the test, which to his youthful imagination was much more than a mere lesson. Had he not tied about his arm the scarlet scarf of his true love? And was she not there, the center of the gay company—Jadwiga, his lady, in her straight, full brocade that shone like the sunlight caught in her hair? Were not the bluest eyes in the kingdom laughing encouragement to him?

So, as spectators enthusiastically approved, he thrust

and parried, tried to smooth his curls behind his ears, and thrust again. There were genuine bravos for his young skill and at the end, calls of, "Valiant Habsburg!" "Brave William!"—for he won—Knight Stephen saw to that.

Then, following all the approved procedure, he ran lightly to his true love to receive the prize—a wreath of leaves and yellow flowers she had gathered and woven herself—which she now merrily awarded. After which old Stoyan, who had fetched his lute, sang in heroic manner a tale of the future exploits of Austria's knight. There were many compliments and affectionate words for the young pair, for whatever one thought of the alliance with Austria none could fail to delight in these two, who pictured in miniature so satisfyingly the romantic ideal of this period.

The lesson over, Jadwiga and William were eager to escape to the base of the hill. At the river's edge they would perhaps discover some new house a beaver or badger had tunneled into the bank during the night. And would count the number of herons sighted above the broad bronze sweep of water, rushing—rushing. Usually they could count on Scribe John or one of their other teacher-friends to accompany them—this day, the historian was delighted to go along. Once beside the river they forgot all but its mystery and might, and the furry and feathered beings that boldly built as near the waters as possible. Here how free they felt; how free they seemed.

Beyond the Danube stretched the vast, fertile Hungarian plain—the plain fed by the river Tisza. They believed they had explored every part of that plain, so dry and dusty in summer; for they had been in their saddles for long hours, day after day. Such riding—the song of the wind in their ears, the rhythm of the race in their blood! For often they sped with terrific wind and sand storms—only those who have given rein to the fiery Arabian pony know what a wind race is. Needless to say, every such adventure bound them in closer comradeship.

Christmas was at Buda, as everywhere, a favorite holiday. And pages and young girls were delighted when they were told that the fun-loving queen mother had promised to spend this Christmas of 1380 with them. None were happier than Jadwiga and William, for whom she had always shown especial affection.

But, alas, as Christmas approached, it was clear that she was so far from well that festivities were not to be thought of. And on December twenty-ninth, the queen wife and mother who had been one of Europe's most picturesque and powerful figures during more than half a century, died. She who had thought nothing of starting forth with her carriage and six horses to cross the continent, would travel no more. Neither young nor old could believe that this was true, it seemed impossible that such vitality should cease.

People would continue to tell tales of her brilliant courts and spectacular excursions. How she had thrilled them, when in '43, knowing her son Andrew in danger in Naples she started in the gold coach for that kingdom, equipped with 27,000 gold marks by Louis, who all but emptied the Visegrád treasury to thus generously supply her. At Zara, in Dalmatia, he had arranged for two boats to meet her, and for two additional war boats contributed by Venice, to conduct her farther by sea.

The 27,000 marks soon dwindled and Louis followed them by 4,000 more. But in Rome (then a city of 17,000 inhabitants, 14,000 of whom were reported beggars!) these too melted so rapidly that the charitable Elizabeth was forced after three days to leave.

She and her following made a great impression on the Italians, whose chronicler remarked that unlike the French, who usually made a scandalous clamor, the Hungarians were always praying and fingering their rosaries. The Latins had grown quickly fond of their royal guest and observing her maimed hand, while they admired her beautiful embroideries, asked how she had been able to achieve them. To which she replied cheerfully that she could now but direct the clever needles as she sat after luncheon with her ladies. When she went to Saint Peter's to see the relics of Saint Peter and Saint Veronica's handkerchief, they spread a long carpet before the portal. And at the end of her brief visit, they saw her depart for Naples with genuine regret.

This independent queen could have requested that her body be laid in the royal burial place, the Cathedral of Székes Fehérvár, which was one of the architectural wonders of the world, but she asked to be buried quietly in the chapel of the nuns of Saint Clara at Buda, whose convent she had founded and supported. Thus she followed her individual desire to the end.

And as characteristic was her will, with its revelation of the warmth and loyalty of her personal relationships. She bequeathed to her son Louis, the only one left of her immediate family, her most precious gold cups, among them a high wine goblet wrought with the figure of Saint Ladislaus and the arms of Hungary and Poland, a gift from Naples. She gave Elizabeth her castle in old Buda, her jewels, and her first prayer book. Mary received a gold chain ornamented with two eagles, and Jadwiga another jewelled chain and a crown encircled with lilies of France. Much was left to members of her court—a prelate, for instance, received four hundred gold florins, a knight three hundred, a page two hundred. To her loved lady-of-honor, Clara, she gave a village, a carriage and six horses, four hundred silver marks, and her second prayer book, which on Clara's death was to go to the nuns of Buda.

Everything remaining after this specified division—all jewels, cups, clothes, furniture, and one thousand gold florins, were to be divided equally among the women of the Hungarian and Polish courts. In addition the pages and courtiers who had no appointments were to receive one thousand florins each and her horses—except the six reserved for her funeral. She left much, too, to the Franciscan, Dominican and Augustinian cloisters in Hungary, and to various churches. And finally she appealed to her daughter-in-law (Elizabeth was one of the executors of her will) to be good to all the women of her court, and to Louis to be equally kind to the men. The will had been written in April, indicating that thus early she suspected the approach of the end and made her preparations.

From all parts of Europe condolences came by courier post to Buda, and they were by no means perfunctory. People knew that in no small measure Louis owed his title of Great to his mother. They recalled many an incident revealing the unusual relationship between mother and son, queen and king. Some still smiled, remembering his letter to the Czech King, the Holy Roman Emperor Charles IV, who during a controversy with Hungary over a demand for indemnities for Czech border robberies, had said, "It is too bad that King Louis allows his mother (using an unlovely epithet) to mix too much in government."

Louis had at once demanded a duel, either with the emperor himself, or between mutual representatives, and this demand being refused, had announced that he would arrive with an army to avenge the insult. In the meantime, he wrote, "We, Louis, by God's grace King of Hungary, to one who calls himself King of the Czechs, send the greetings he deserves. Who offends the source of honor, does not deserve to be honored; who cannot control himself, ought not to control others. Can you rule over territories, who cannot rule over your own bad tongue?

"What manner of King are you, whose King, Wine, leads you to dishonor a lady whom the whole world respects? Did you but think of yourself as born of the honest womb of your mother, you would respect women and not speak thus of them. Had you lived virtuously, you would not thus in drunkenness defame her Majesty, my mother.

"I commend you to take back your calumny, and before all to praise my mother to the extent that you have slandered her. Otherwise you will feel our revenge, for we will defend our mother's honor and our own honor!"

Here sounded the note of his vigorous devotion. What would Louis do without his mother? That he himself was ill was an open secret. No one thought that his wife could take his mother's place in counsel or in practical participation in his government. Yet it was but natural that despite her genuine grief, Elizabeth now jubilantly hoped that at last she might win the position from which her mother-in-law's superior gifts and experience had so long barred her.

But for the moment her first duty was to comfort the king and to provide for Jadwiga and Mary and the other young people some relief from the gloom of the long and black court mourning. She decided early to take them in canoes to Saint Margaret's Island lying in the Danube just below, a trip neither she nor they ever tired of repeating.

Saint Margaret's story touched them all concretely. For her father, the Magyar King Béla IV, had built their home, the Visegrád tower palace, in her memory, the queen giving her jewels to help. Later the splendid church of Saint Margaret and the cloisters of the Dominican nuns on this neighboring island had risen to commemorate her great renunciation. For she had left the glamor and ease of her father's court to become a nun and had so devoted her life to holy works, that ever since her death miracles had been wrought in her name. Her island was one of the best-loved pilgrimage spots of Europe. Entire villages had sprung up on it.

In Jadwiga's imagination, so quickly stirred by mystical beauty, Saint Margaret was especially glorified. She herself had been named after the Polish Saint Jadwiga who lived in the preceding century.

Scribe John had narrated to his pupils again and again each step in Saint Margaret's progress, and with each telling had restressed its moral that service is the highest aim of life. He was always endeavoring to build for them an historical background for the ideal of sacrifice, for his presentation of life as a passing spectacle, in which the only enduring things are won from contemplation and dedication of oneself to others. In Hungary one felt the influence of the East, of people who think in categories of centuries.

Queen Elizabeth had her own miniature reception

palace on Saint Margaret's island as King Louis and the Archbishop of Estergom and others had theirs. And to its comfortable plastered chamber with the corner fire-place she first conducted her troop, depending chiefly on Lady-in-waiting Priscilla and young Elizabeth to keep them properly together. Which was not too easy, for they would have postponed prayers for an immediate excursion down half the length of the island (it was over a mile long) past the Franciscan monastery to the hot sulphur springs. There it was fascinating to watch steam and hot water welling apparently directly from the cold Danube—the island seemed but floating on the river.

After refreshing themselves in the palace, in through the famous golden portal of the church they went, and kneeling on the red marble pavement, told their beads before the white marble altar and the low grave of Saint Margaret. A service was in progress and they knew that the sisters were following it from behind the windows of the oratorium beyond. There was something movingly mysterious about the complete invisibility of these nuns who were hovering all about and following everything from all sorts of apertures.

When the service was ended they crossed the cloister-surrounded court, abloom with big centifoglia roses and lilies, stopping, as they always did, to admire the fountain whose waters flowed into nine marble shells where nine at a time, the nuns could separately wash their hands. Then they continued to the refectory. There, after washing their own hands in the lava basin at the entrance, they hungrily settled themselves on the board-covered stone benches following the walls, before the heaps of sandwiches and cakes piled on the long narrow tables. As they ate, Queen Elizabeth described the way in which at meal times the youngest nuns ate first, and the Prioress, emulating the humility of Saint Margaret, last. Observing that, of course, being polite, the novices always restrained their natural appetites and left the best for their superior!

The refectory was heated by hot air from fires below the floor so that it was always comfortable. As was the hospital which the queen now went to inspect, and where she comforted the sick who had come from far and near with her faith in Saint Margaret's power and in the virtues of the waters to cure them.

While she was there, the young people were at last free to enjoy bathing and swimming. In the late afternoon when they reluctantly got ready to return, the great bronze bell of the church was ringing. They had read its inscription,

"Help us God and Mary,
Us simple people."

The sun was hanging low beyond Buda Hill as they crossed the river.

CHAPTER VI

King Louis Dies

Not long after the excursion to Saint Margaret's Island, Louis called to Buda the leaders of the Polish state and church that they might "through a healing decision restore order." In the spring of 1381, once again, while the people hoped, their masters assembled. And once again disillusioned, the people heard that the "healing decision" was the appointment by Louis of a triumvirate to rule their distracted country. They were far from reassured, because no one of the men selected had in the past proved himself strong enough to dominate the situation.

Now that he had disposed of difficulties in Poland, at least for the moment, the king turned to other matters. He began preparations for a journey to northern Hungary. He wanted to live for a time in his castle at Dios Györ, one of his favorite hunting strongholds. But he was not planning to hunt the boars and stags and bears of this lower Carpathian mountain country during this visit. He would hold courts and attend to regional state matters, but chiefly he wished to think and to talk with the Benedictines of the nearby monastery. He had already sent word to Venice that the mission she was about to send north, must meet him there. And his own suite, the Bishops of Pécs, Zagreb and Warod, and the Bans of Ruthenia, Dalmatia and Croatia, along with a cavalcade of knights, were getting ready to accompany him.

Jadwiga wished greatly that she might be allowed to go along. Her father had once taken her and William and the family with him to this beautiful estate when he went there to hunt. She remembered the great walls squaring the hilltop, their corner towers, which one sighted across the exquisitely green rolling country so long before reaching them, and the rugged palace within the walled enclosure. By day she and William had explored fern-filled valleys and pine woods, and gathered tiger lilies and wood orchids till they could gather no more, and at night they had been thrilled by recitals of the battles and victories of the chase. But she knew that there was no hope of repeating that visit at this time.

The trip up the broad Tisza River Valley to Dios Györ and the quiet days of living again in the pure northern air were almost immediately bracing, and King Louis welcomed the Venetian envoys, Leonard Dandolo and George Fantino, in good spirits.

Moreover, the Italian mission could not have pleased him better than by bringing him, as they did, the holy relics of Saint Paul as a gift. He was greatly moved, and after the successful conclusion of the conference and of his visit, he carried the sacred treasure back to Buda and deposited it in the chapel of Saint John in Buda Castle. Later, in a gorgeous procession whose preparation the young people followed during many days, the king himself marched with the bishops and officers of the realm, as the relics were carried from the castle to the nearby cloister of the order of Saint Paul.

The new treaty with Venice was for Louis the outstanding event of this year. By it the Island Republic relinquished all claims to Dalmatia, and in addition agreed to pay Hungary on Saint Stephen's Day an annual tribute of seven thousand ducats. Neither victor nor vanquished realized that this was to prove their last important negotiation.

Busy chroniclers were setting down these events, though they were apt to give much more space to military successes than to those of peaceful progress. They gloried in Louis' brilliant victories in the wars against Naples and in accounts of his crusades against the Turks and Lithuanians. Later history, however, was to acclaim this great king's social and economic achievements. Indeed, certain discriminating contemporaries already praised chiefly his administrative ability and his exercise of justice. Petrarch wrote of him that he possessed four great virtues; intelligence, justice, energy, self-control. And John, Patriarch of Alexandria, sent by the Holy See on a mission to Hungary, reported, "I have never seen a King who combined so much might with so much modesty."

The closing weeks of 1381 were especially filled with arrivals and departures of envoys and visitors.

On one day strangers from Dalmatia, who came, suntanned and dust-covered, their brown travelling capes and gold loop earrings a like powdery gray, brought not alone gifts for the king and queen but also a mysterious packet of green leaves for the princesses. The pages and girls could scarcely wait until the reception and welcoming speeches and replies were over (they often found these boring) to discover what this packet might contain. "That a princess may observe the spinners of her fine robes," said its bearer gaily, as he spread apart the mulberry leaves and revealed a colony of silk worms. "They will not like this northern climate, but at least they will live long enough for you to see a miracle performed." There was breathless excitement and a volley of questions as they crowded about the leafy bed, which they finally bore outdoors, where there were superior opportunities for investigation.

As month followed month, King Louis was less and less interested in such comings and goings. He was fixing his attention on his own last journey. And he gave all the time he could spare from internal affairs, —from the crisis that again threatened in Poland and the old and disturbing necessity of watching ambitious Naples—to contemplation, and to the society of his most learned priests. He was now trying to put an ever widening distance between himself and that pomp and glory which his own great qualities had called into being. He wanted to define his position in the next world which he felt now to be not far distant. "The more the Lord raised him, the more humble he was."

In July of 1382, knowing his strength waning, he summoned all the Polish governors of provinces to a conference in his northern hunting castle at Zólym. There they would discuss conditions in their troubled country, and agree again to the accession of Mary and Sigismund. He knew that in this assembly he would face a divided loyalty and an uncertain enthusiasm. But when the delegates were assembled and he ordered them to declare for Sigismund, they did so! Secretly the opposition had not yielded. Yet the Poles longed honestly for a settlement, and above all for a strong king, present and not absent.

The powerful of Europe were closely watching the closing scenes of the Hungarian drama. King Louis was only fifty-six, but his mentally brilliant and vigorous Anjevin line was short-lived. Fine and strong-looking they were, yet they were curiously lacking in physical stamina; or else their capacities led them to an expenditure of strength that wrecked bodies which might otherwise have attained the allotted three-score years and ten. As it was, Louis had outlived all his brothers. His mother had had the Polish Piasts' enduring vitality.

All sorts of rumors flashed from court to court and people to people. One said that the king had, sometime before, on one of his southeastern campaigns, contracted the dread leprosy. Else why should he lately keep so apart from men? Another that he remained so long away from Buda only because of a growing asceticism—that he was about to assemble the representatives of his entire realm, resign his crown and retire for good to a monastery.

That his over-strenuous life had sapped his strength until there was not enough left to carry the responsibilities of government for so vast a realm, he knew better than anyone else, better even than Doctor Radlica who had been so close to him. He owed much, he felt, to King Charles of France, for when he had written asking Charles to send him a physician, the French king had dispatched the rather short, unimpressive Pole, John Radlica, who had been educated at Montpellier. And from the day of his arrival at Buda his devotion and skill had made him invaluable to Louis. Temperamentally, too, John was most sympathetic, for he was simple and direct—no courtier—calm, a peace-maker in all quarrels. Now Louis felt that it might have been better had he kept Doctor Radlica beside him and not sent him as Chancellor to Krakow.

When the time neared for the return to Buda, the king decided to ride homeward, not along the direct route down the Tisza Valley, but by way of the northeast where he had further work to do. With a limited suite he left his castle at Dios Györ and travelled toward the Austrian frontier. But on reaching Nagy Zombat he felt so weak and ill that no work was to be thought of, and he halted his journey to rest in a private house. In the quiet of a large, plain, gray vaulted chamber he tried to regain his strength and to compose his mind. Each day, however, found him weaker, until his case seemed indeed hopeless. Messengers hurried to Buda to summon Queen Elizabeth and Mary and Jadwiga, and the traditional officials of Church and state. And the pale king waited, holding the crucifix to his breast, while attendants came and went and the constant murmur of prayers for the dying filled the room. Many flickering candles gave its austere lines a solemn beauty.

No wonder that Europe, awed and amazed, fixed its thought on that frontier room. The Anjevin Louis, son of Charles Robert, and one of the most brilliant personalities of the century, lay dying in a private house off near the border of his land! Not at Buda in the midst of all he had so laboriously and successfully constructed. This was, it is true, a time of wandering and detachment, but the great Louis should finish his work in his capital, in his own palace, surrounded by those he loved and on whom he had always depended, and cared for by the queen who had been for thirty years not only his royal mate but his comrade.

Elizabeth and Mary were the first to reach Nagy Zombat. Sigismund was in the north fighting in the Polish province of Mazovia, against its duke who was trying to seize the Polish crown before it should be given to another. The magnates, despite all their hurrying, arrived too late. How touching were the scenes at the royal bedside in that far, gray room—the parting between the king and queen, the husband and wife, whose marriage had been a true love match, the last words of counsel, the last expressions of faith. None were ever to forget them while they lived. And least of all, Jadwiga, who worshipped her father—she had been called from Vienna. As she and William knelt for the last time beside him, faintly but clearly, he again affirmed their heaven-appointed union, and gave them his final blessing.

Elizabeth and the three young people knelt, all close together near their king and loved one—a strangely pathetic little group on whom a glorious but heavy heritage now descended. The end came a little before midnight on September 12th. As they kissed the crucifix it was bathed in their tears.

The body was taken first to Buda where during six days of almost overwhelming ceremonies, awed throngs of high and low degree converged on the capital. From mountain sides brilliant in their early autumn coloring and plains glowing with the harvest, they poured into the black city. Many thousand wax candles burned themselves out, and the intoned Latin of masses and singing and the chanting of choirs seemed never to cease. Finally, the coffin was transported in the state carriage heavy with black and drawn by many horses, to the magnificent cathedral at Székes Fehérvár, southeast of the capital, and there laid in the chapel of Saint Catherine, which Louis himself had built. The culminating solemnities were broken by the weeping of the queen and Mary and Jadwiga and by that of many others present. Foreboding mingled with grief, for preceding Louis' death a comet had streamed across the heavens—of what coming disaster was it the flaming presage?

A three years' mourning was decreed throughout the land. Sorrow was deep and real. People said that they felt as if they themselves were dead.

CHAPTER VII

Poland Turns to Jadwiga

A brief five years before Hungary buried King Louis with all the mystical splendor of Catholic ritual, while Rome asked, "Who will replace my son, Rex Christianissimus?" far in the Baltic north beyond immense marshes and forests, there was another royal burial. There had died Duke Olgierd, ruler of the last pagan people of Europe; those outcast Lithuanians against whom both William's uncle and King Louis had joined the Knights of the Cross in a crusade. And just as to Christian Hungarians it seemed impossible that King Louis had died, so to pagan Lithuanians it seemed impossible that Duke Olgierd was dead.

Nobody knew whence these Lithuanians had come or exactly when. They were a yellow-haired, blue-eyed people of Indo-European origin, with whom some strong dark race had in the past united. Their language showed kinship with Sanscrit. Western rulers could scarcely credit the size of their possessions, the achievement of a series of warrior leaders culminating in Olgierd. Profiting by the break-up of the early Russian principalities, they had conquered almost all of White and Little Russia from Smolensk to Kiev. It had been impossible, however, to consolidate these enormous dependencies stretching along the Dneiper River from the Baltic to the Black Sea, for they had no common culture. So that it was not strange that about them should come violently conflicting accounts. Their remote peoples were described by some as savages, heathen idolators, living in wigwams, fierce in war and cruel at all times; by others as intelligent and powerful, patterning their lives after that of Olgierd's brother, the greatly loved Duke Kiejstut, a pagan Arthurian Knight to his people. He had, it is true, run away with one of the virgins who tended the sacred fire. But he was so staunch a pagan that the people, and even the powerful hierarchy of priests, overlooked his marriage with Biruta.

Statesmen, it appeared, could spring from unholy as from holy soil. For with constructive foresight, Lithuanian dukes were envisaging the growth of a clearly determined empire out of the vast precariously held territories of eastern Europe. Alone the "White Capes" of the Baltic marshes, loosing their bloodhounds and kindling their fires on Lithuania's western frontier, threatened to block the achievement of the pagan builders' dream.

Just as Louis in succeeding Charles Robert, so Olgierd in succeeding Gedymin, followed a father who had laid the foundation of a greater state. And out of pagan darkness Olgierd and Kiejstut had given incredulous Europe an example of a harmonious double rule hardly to be matched in Christian annals. At the start, they had agreed that Olgierd should be titular ruler. Then they divided their two major tasks. Kiejstut was to be chiefly responsible for defense in the west, which meant meeting the fierce pressure of the German Knights; while Olgierd would give his first attention to Lithuania's advance into Russ territory where the Tatars fled before him as sheep before the wolf. For almost half a century these two "outcasts" demonstrated the possibility of such affectionate fraternal cooperation.

Now, Olgierd, empire builder, lay dead. He had twice married Ruthenian princesses of the orthodox faith and like other grand dukes allowed his Christian wives private chapels and freedom to worship in their own way. With a consenting opportunism he had even been baptized before his death. But his pagan people knew him to be pagan still. So, in Vilno, his capital, they carried him to the ancient sanctuary. In the forest of Kokiveithus, where priests guarded the sacred oaks and the serpents in whom their gods lived, and where death awaited the trespasser, they laid his body, clad in a red and gold robe and jewelled belt and a coat sown with pearls and gems, on the enormous funeral pyre. Then they brought his favorite horse and dogs and falcons to be burned with him. And while white robed virgins assisted, the high priest offered sacrifices and poured milk and hydromel upon the altar. Strange chanting echoed through the dark forest as the pyre was lighted.

No less grief-stricken than the Bosnian Elizabeth at Buda, Olgierd's Ruthenian wife, Julianna, surrounded by her many warrior sons, watched the consuming flames. The seventh son, Jagiello, the Lucky, was to succeed his father.

This pagan funeral intensely interested not only terrorized Tatars and Poles, but the German Knights, greedy for Lithuanian lands, and Rome, which had for so long prayed that the lost sheep of the north might be brought into the fold, had so often hoped that the great King Louis might consummate that victory. Now both the powerful pagan of the north and the powerful Christian of the south were gone. . . .

Despite the strength of the guarantees which King Louis had set so securely about the betrothal of William and Jadwiga, William's father at once sought their renewal. Poland, Venice, Austria,—all were seething with dynastic problems and intrigues; no one could look far ahead. Duke Leopold determined to keep in closest touch with the progress of events at Buda. He felt certain that however loyally Queen Elizabeth might appear to wish to carry out the king's desires, he must count her not friend, but enemy. Fortunately, William would soon reach his majority; he determined to press for the marriage even before that time.

Many Hungarian magnates were already prophesying disaster as the result of a female regency; for it was clear that Elizabeth would, at least for a time, rule for both daughters. To prevent an interregnum Mary had been crowned the day after her father's funeral.

She had been crowned with the crown of Saint Stephen, King—Maria Rex. Yet it was hard for Hungary, which had not before had a female ruler, to accept a queen. People looked to the day when William would bring to the empire the strength of Austria, and Sigismund the prestige of the Holy Roman Empire. And they resolved to hasten that day.

After the death of the queen mother, Louis had more and more consulted his wife. She had certain gifts, and great ambition. Through the years when she had been forced to remain in the background, she had longed for the opportunity to prove her powers. But being consulted and playing a second role of intriguante was, after all, vastly different from carrying the real and enormous responsibility of administration. So far the motive power of her life had been her love for the king. She had trusted him and let him act for her. During all the years of her mother-in-law's predominance, her great virtue had been flexibility—that had had to be her method. Could she now become hard and wise and strong? How would she find a diplomacy that would hold that star of her crown, Dalmatia, secure? And hold difficult Ruthenia, united with Poland under Casimir, and unruly Croatia, as well? What of the relations between the Anjous of Hungary and those of Naples, with Charles, king there, and Louis dead? True, Charles had sworn loyalty to Louis' wife and daughters, but could Charles of Durazzo be trusted?

Furthermore, not all magnates had approved King

Louis' policy of unlimited encouragement of his cities. Such strength they viewed as a menace to their own. Would Elizabeth gather about her those who would encourage or check their growth? Though in this century women enjoyed a position of great respect, even reverence, this need not necessarily extend to enthusiasm over a rule of petticoats, or even to confidence in it. So they objected and conspired.

Queen Elizabeth and her children longed for the peace and beauty of Visegrád during the somber, late fall weather, but for the present there could be no thought of returning to Eagles' Nest. Buda was the more logical administrative center of the Kingdom, more generally accessible than Visegrád. So while the preparation of Jadwiga and Mary was being pushed in every possible way, the queen found herself almost continually in conference in the palace on Buda Hill. Into the gloom of official and personal mourning arrived mission after mission.

Jadwiga, swept by passionate grief, could not believe that her adored father, her constant teacher, was no longer there to guide her. If only he might have lived till she had reached her majority! William sorrowed with her, for Louis had been for him, too, a loved father and teacher. Scribe John was one of the most comforting friends they had at this time. He was working day and night now on his history of King Louis' reign. He stirred the gold dust and the colored powders in the little metal and earthenware pots and painted in the exquisite pictures more ardently than ever before. They visited his workshop whenever they could and always he would turn from his task to cheer them with an amusing tale.

During these initial critical days, the chief figures of the court rallied about Elizabeth. The Bishop of Veszprem, her physician as well as her spiritual and political adviser, was constantly near. But she depended most upon that old, tried family friend, Nicholas of Gara, a man of many resources but also of many enemies, to whom her husband had given the highest position of the realm. Despite such aid and counsel, and despite her own optimistic temperament, the queen regent, as she faced a circle of dangers, even during the first months, could not escape hours of doubt and fear.

The problem of Poland was more urgent than any other. King Louis had died after a reign of forty years in Hungary, where he had won fame and honor, and of twelve years in Poland, where he had won neither. In those twelve years he had visited his northern kingdom but seldom. And as an inevitable result of such neglect many of the solid achievements of his uncle, Casimir the Great, were breaking down. In the absence of a strong hand, and distracted by the struggles of turbulent princes, Poland seemed to be falling to pieces.

The people had been extremely fond of Louis' mother, their queen regent, and proud to see visitors flocking to her court, which she had made a mecca for poets and artists of all kinds. They appreciated her encouragement of the growth of cities and of the development of Poland's economic resources, though they could not yet picture the approaching century of flourishing commerce and industry, due in no small measure to her efforts. They realized that if she neglected some things, it was not because of indolence, but for lack of time. Especially in all matters directly touching the dynasty, she did what she could. The Pacts of Kassa (signed in '73 and '74) in which the Polish throne was pledged to a daughter of Louis had been largely her work. But her efforts had not saved the land from civil strife and its attendant misery.

It was only when she was nearing seventy that this extraordinary old lady had at last seen the folly of her optimism. And when news of a fresh Lithuanian invasion and another bloody clash between Hungarians and Poles overwhelmed her, she decided, with sadness and anxiety, to leave Krakow and put the army in stronger hands. She hurried to Hungary, and Louis led soldiers across the Carpathians to punish offenders and regain lost power. It was then that he had established a triumvirate in Krakow in the hope of averting further confusion. But this had proved a vain hope. And when Elizabeth returned, it was to a country moving fast toward chaos.

Excuse for King Louis' disastrous policy is discoverable in the fact that Poland formed but a small part of his vast dominions. Poland's interests had to be subordinated to the larger demands of an imperial policy that embraced half Europe within its orbit.

However, to the suffering Poles this was no justification. The truth was that there had never been a close bond between Louis and his Polish subjects. They had quite naturally resented his estimate of their culture as inferior to that of his own people. And it had not been difficult for him to yield to pressure of nearer duties and leave Poland chiefly to the care of others.

Conditions in Poland now called for quick action. To be sure, the magnates had more than once pledged their loyalty to King Louis' plan that Mary and Sigismund should inherit the Polish crown. Only two months before his death, they had repeated this pledge. But the prospect of Sigismund as king had never stirred enthusiasm, even among Louis' supporters. Recently this fourteen year old prince had appeared in Poland under the leadership of Archbishop Bodzanta and Palatin Sedziwosz and others and with his army had tried to overcome those opposed to his candidacy. But he had not succeeded. Not only had he too swiftly turned away envoys who asked him to pledge himself to live in Poland, but he had also persistently refused to dismiss an officer whom the Poles particularly disliked, had failed to invite Poles to sit at his table, and had in other ways offended them. Since that time they had doubly regretted their promises. Daily it seemed more certain that the rising wave of opposition would bar Mary and Sigismund from the throne.

Then, in November, at Radom in Great Poland, the controlling nobles definitely decided that Sigismund should not hold their scepter. It was imperative that their king should live in Poland, and obviously Sigismund would not since his fiancée, Mary, had already been crowned Queen of Hungary. These Polish nobles were through with absentee rulers. And, after terrible experiences with the Teutonic Knights, entrenched beyond their northern frontier, they wanted no German at their head. They dismissed the question of the wrong they might do Mary in breaking their promises to King Louis, and determined to make their own choice. Asserting their privilege to select the successor within the reigning family, they would, while remaining true to the Anjevins, reject Mary, and turn to Louis' second daughter, Jadwiga, who must, on coming to them, agree to remain forever in Poland. Unfortunately, Jadwiga was also betrothed to a German prince. But neither she nor William had yet quite reached their majorities—they would take care of William! From now on they would demand Jadwiga!

CHAPTER VIII

A Mother's Desperate Battle for Time

Despite his efforts, then, King Louis had left his kingdom in a perilous position. Jadwiga, not yet of age, Mary only twelve, Elizabeth at fifty still beautiful, charming and eager to prove that she possessed capacities hitherto unrecognized, but nevertheless commanding little confidence—these were to steer the threatened ship of state. There seemed to be little hope for a steady course, with Elizabeth as pilot.

She had position and power at last; but already how distractingly more complicated than she had expected, was her task. There were plots and counterplots on all sides, many of them centering on Nicholas of Gara. Certain powerful nobles above him in birth, who had long resented his position of influence with the Anjevin family, believed their chance to unseat him had arrived. But it was not jealousy of Nicholas, nor the danger in Hungary's relations with Venice, with the province of Ruthenia, and with Naples, not the many other political problems, that made the queen look from Buda Hill across the marvelous panorama of ridges and river and plain into a world dark with uncertainty.

It was the fact that beneath all political ambition

ran the stronger current of her mother love. What was in store for Mary and Jadwiga? She had won a coveted position only through bitter bereavement. Was she to pay the added price of her children's happiness? There were nights when she gathered them in her arms in a very panic of apprehension. However, from too many such hours a natural light-heartedness and optimism rescued her. Also, her religion sustained her. As perplexities multiplied she prayed more frequently before the Madonna above the prie-dieu in her chamber and before the crucifix in the royal chapel.

She felt that her course would have been much clearer had King Louis but chosen other sons-in-law. She appreciated the growing importance of the Brandenburg and Habsburg houses, and her husband's reasoning in making his grave double decision. But she found Sigismund unsympathetic—their differences already made Mary unhappy—she would postpone that marriage as long as possible. And she was still unreconciled to the Austrian alliance.

Sigismund, who had gone to Poland with an army to claim the throne, had been forced to return to Hungary before even reaching the capital. Indeed, every report from Poland made it increasingly clear that the Slavs were steadfastly determined not to accept him as king and Mary as queen.

Well, if the inheritances had to be exchanged Elizabeth felt she would not find that too difficult. She had never abandoned the hope of dropping William; in this transfer her opportunity might lie. She would agree to the Poles' proposal. But there could be no question of parting now with Jadwiga. Send her beautiful younger daughter, not yet of age, not yet prepared, to Poland? She knew too well the dangers in that disordered country. She remembered that her mother-in-law had fled after the massacre of over one hundred and fifty Hungarians who had sought refuge in the royal chateau at Krakow. Never would her mind be at peace, with Jadwiga, so young, holding a scepter of such uncertain potentialities. It would have been safer to send Mary; but Mary was, after all, more needed in Hungary. She must be clever enough to hold fast to the Polish crown and at the same time to her child! Whereupon Elizabeth launched one of the most amazing games of royal hide and seek ever witnessed.

She was almost constantly in consultation with one of her advisers or with the whole royal council over other matters, but her passionate concern centered always on this mother's battle with Poland. Back and forth across the northern border hurtled promises and explanations, galloped messengers and envoys. Meetings were held, courts assembled. From the Pope and the Holy Emperor down, all the arbiters of Europe had their parts in the game; for chaos in Poland invited meddling on all sides.

The young people at Buda knew little of these happenings. Their life continued much as it had been before, though Mary and Jadwiga saw their mother less frequently now, and often felt her preoccupation when she was with them. They knew that she was struggling to keep them all together and they strove to prove to her that they understood.

Jadwiga's teachers, Scribe John, the Bishop of Veszprem and the others, kept close to her during these crucial months, and while pushing her studies, yearned over her with protecting affection. To the pages and girls at court, the romantic aspect of the drama was thrilling. Their Jadza, to travel to far Poland, to be queen over millions of people—if only Queen Elizabeth would arrange for them all to go along as escort! At least as far as Dios Györ, or Kassa. They envied Elizabeth, daughter of the governor of Ruthenia whose family had been very close to King Louis, for unquestionably she would be one of those to accompany their princess to Krakow. King Louis had arranged Elizabeth's marriage with a handsome young Polish knight, Spytko, of another family which had loyally supported him. In Krakow Spytko and Elizabeth would be the young queen's intimate friends. At times, Jadwiga, too, caught her companions' romantic enthusiasm, but mostly she clung to the thought that her mother would succeed, and that if she had to go away from her home to an unknown land, it would not be until she and William were married, and could go together.

Next to the game of selecting the accompanying cavalcade, none was more engrossing than that of choosing the treasure Jadwiga should take with her.

The great wooden travel chests stood ready to be filled—the queen regent, though counting on her skill in evasion, felt it wise to be prepared for any emergency. These chests were splendidly adequate to serve a princess and prospective queen, with their fine iron locks, their carving and painting, and the Magyar and Anjevin arms in relief. Inside they were all musk and rose scent.

There were pretty scenes, when, forgetting their common sorrow, and the heavy cares of royalty, mother and daughters, with their closest friends about them, bent over patterns and colors, deciding between this or that brocade or fur, as happy as girls together. Often someone teasingly demanded of Jadwiga William's ideas as to what would be most becoming to a queen and his bride—he had returned for a time to his father's court. Scarcely a week passed without somebody's thinking of another article to be folded away in a Krakow chest.

Anna, Jadwiga's short, plump, unfailingly good-natured governess-companion, spent most of her day bustling to and from the room where the wardrobe was being assembled. She would, of course, go with her princess. The queen regent and Queen Mary realized that with Jadwiga far away, they would find greatest comfort in the thought of Anna's watchful care. They were cheered, too, by the Bishop of Veszprem's promise to present her with a section of the horn of a unicorn which Jadwiga was to wear about her neck as protection from harm. Several of the nearby monasteries possessed such coveted treasures, which detected poisons and cured ills.

The touching scenes at Buda were being paid for in misery. At Krakow—in all Poland—what tragedy of disunion! Finally, with the breach between the nobles of Great Poland and those of Small Poland ever widening, and with civil war an actuality, the magnates desperately determined to end Elizabeth's maneuvering. If Jadwiga were not to be sent to them, they would proceed to choose a king. They called a great meeting at Sieradz, to assemble in the church there toward the close of February, 1383. There they would officially declare the succession.

The queen regent sent her trusted counsellors Nicholas of Gara and the Bishop of Veszprem and two other Hungarian nobles to represent her at this meeting. They were to speak in her name, and while lamenting the results of the strife between rival factions in Poland, were to insist on her right under their agreement with King Louis, to name one of his daughters to be their queen. She would gladly have sent Mary, but since that was now impossible, she released them from all promises they had formerly made to Mary and Sigismund. And, following their already expressed wish, she would send them Louis' younger daughter, provided, however, that the Poles would unqualifiedly promise to let her return after her coronation, for three years longer with her mother.

It was a stormy session. Bodzanta, keen-eyed, influential Archbishop of Gnesen, leader of the Polish legitimist party, which was made up chiefly of magnates of Great Poland who wished the Piast line restored, directed the opposition to an Anjevin ruler. He was there to see Ziemowit of the Piast line elected. This Duke of the feudal province of Mazovia was the strongest prince in Poland. Incidentally, no Slavs were physically more superb than these Mazovians; it was said that even their women could snap an iron bar in their hands.

In a sonorous voice Bodzanta asked, "Do you want Ziemowit of Mazovia as king?" "Yes," shouted his followers, "we want him and we beg you to crown him!"

But up jumped Jasko of Tenczyn, long a loyal supporter of Louis, and after calling for quiet, began to speak. "Noble men and brothers," he said, "it is not seemly that we be overhasty in this choice. We are bound to keep faith with Jadwiga, the daughter of Louis. If she will come to us at Easter, agreeing to live with her husband in our country and to rule here as queen, we will welcome her. Otherwise, we will choose a king. We have given the dead King Louis this promise and strengthened it by letter and by seal." Thus, amidst tremendous applause and excitement, he swung the delegates to the support of Jadwiga. They declared her queen, and requested that she come to them at Pentecost (six weeks after Easter) to be crowned. Nicholas Gara and the Bishop of Veszprem and the others hurried back to Buda with their report of the meeting.

At Pentecost, the great nobles of all parties in Poland flocked to Sandec, nearer the border than Krakow, to welcome the queen mother and her daughter. Archbishop Bodzanta went with them, which was not surprising, but it was surprising that he should be accompanied by five hundred well-armed men. And above all, why concealed in their midst should ride Duke Ziemowit, the most powerful rival aspirant for the crown?

All quarters buzzed with rumors of a plot. The Archbishop and the Duke planned to return to Krakow before the others, to hold it with armed men, and on Jadwiga's arrival, seize her, marry her to Ziemowit, and crown them together, king and queen!

Although there were neither telephone nor radio in those days, secrets escaped then as now, speeding by plume and stirrup. Krakow was warned, and the good burghers, mostly Germans, got ready to lock the gates against the plotters. And Queen Elizabeth, who had reluctantly started with Jadwiga, and journeyed northward up the Tisza Valley as far as Kassa now saw Fate again playing into her hands. At Kassa she had encountered the spring floods and had decided that the waters might serve as sufficient excuse for a retreat, but now she saw two roads of escape!

She despatched messengers to Sandec to report that since, unfortunately, floods prevented her from proceeding farther, she hoped that the Poles would send representatives to Kassa to discuss her difficult position with her. Which they did! Castellan Dobieslaw, Spytko of Meltzyn, Sedziwosz of Zubina and other officials came, and after reviewing in detail the decisions of the meeting at Sieradz, and discussing the situation from all sides—in particular the dangers of the Bodzanta-Ziemowit kidnapping plot—they finally accepted a further postponement. Jadwiga was to come to them definitely in November. Furthermore, they agreed that if she were to die without heirs the Polish crown would go to Mary; and that if Mary should die childless, the Hungarian crown was to go to Poland, an arrangement which ran counter to the desires of both peoples.

After this conference the representatives returned to the north, the great nobles bearing many gifts, and the lesser ones, as usual, without fruits. This was in May, and by November, the negotiators believed, Ziemowit would have been obliged to occupy himself with affairs in his dukedom. Sigismund was preparing to invade it from the south, with twelve thousand Hungarians reinforced by troops from Krakow and Sandomir. And from the northeast the dread Jagiello, ruler of Lithuania, was ready to cross the frontier to harry and destroy. In addition, the Teutonic Knights might, by November, have withdrawn the support which Elizabeth charged they were furnishing Ziemowit.

But these eventualities were still in the future. Actually, the Mazovian considered himself as good as crowned. Having advanced as far as the church of

Saint Florian near Krakow, and had the gates of the city shut before him, he was planning his next move when a delegation of Krakovians appeared to appeal to him to retire without harming the capital. This he agreed to do, and at Korezin, waited for news from Kassa. If necessary, he would watch the frontier, and kidnap Jadwiga, as she crossed it!

While he waited, the queen regent, with intense relief and secret rejoicing, was hurrying with her daughter back along the Tisza Valley to Buda. The whole adventure was replete with thrills,—a superlatively comic performance if one could forget the helpless millions in the background. And if one could forget Jadwiga.

Six months' reprieve—what joy on Buda Hill! And, alas, what a growing network of intrigue at court, where the queen regent, following first this and then that bad counsel, allowed herself to get increasingly entangled. That flexibility which had so long served her well was now leading her to the brink of a precipice.

In November of 1383, as Saint Martin's day approached, all Poland looked toward Hungary, whence Louis' daughter, who was to rescue the land from the unholy disorder into which it had fallen, would come. Many watched with misgiving, which was justified. The day arrived, but no queen came. For once again Elizabeth broke her promise.

The governor of Krakow, Sedziwosz, decided to go in person to Buda, taking with him Jasko, castellan of Sandomir, and several other officials, all desperately determined this time to put an end to the queen's perfidies. When they arrived they found that she had left for Zara in Dalmatia, to quell a disturbance there. And to Zara the governor of Krakow and his suite followed her!

From the first he was apprehensive. Elizabeth received him coolly; their interviews did not progress smoothly. She sent Jasko back to Krakow with the request that the capital hill and the city be turned over to Hungarian troops stationed in Poland. Whereupon Sedziwosz managed to send a messenger to warn the Poles. "Even if you hear they are burning me alive, do not turn Krakow over to Hungarian troops," he wrote. Then, fearing imprisonment, he himself fled to Krakow and by relays reached there before his messenger! Elizabeth's anger flamed. In retaliation, she imprisoned his cousins and several other Polish nobles.

It is not difficult to imagine the impression that reports of these happenings made in Poland. The nobles met on March second of this year 1384, at Radom, and decided to send their final ultimatum to Hungary, this time by a soldier! Brave Wanwelski would carry it. The queen regent was to produce Princess Jadwiga within two months, or a king would be chosen. Moreover, no single other embassy would be sent to Hungary. But despite this declaration, there were further delays and another envoy did go to Buda—Spytek of Tarnovo—before Elizabeth, convinced that further equivocation meant certain defeat, capitulated.

She had been fighting for time and had gained two years; fighting also for the concession, that once crowned, Jadwiga would continue her education at Buda. This, largely because the Poles distrusted her motive, she had lost. Those watching with anxiety her unsteady course, even those most devoted to her, thought of how differently—with how much surer hand, either King Louis or his mother would have fought this amazing battle of the Polish succession.

And now the limit of time neared; Poland rang with war cries. Very soon Elizabeth's child, but King Louis' daughter and Poland's queen, must depart from Buda.

CHAPTER IX

The Hegira

The morning of departure approached. Despite sadness and inner fears, Jadwiga was lovelier than ever. The lambent blue of her eyes, the changing tints of her glowing skin and sunny hair, gave her a jewel-like beauty. Polish ambassadors to her mother's court returned to report that they had been struck dumb by her appearance and by her unexpected maturity and gravity and charm—for she had an ineffable quality which captivated everyone who came near her.

How much she and William knew of all that had been passing, we can only conjecture. But whatever perils ahead their young imaginations conjured up, they faced them with a fine confidence from the sure ground of their inviolable betrothal pact. Had either suspected that there would not be a speedy reunion in Krakow, these days before their parting would have been different. They were sad enough as it was. The lovers refused to be separated, taking long farewell rides together and spending other free hours during the final days of preparation for the long journey, in revisiting favorite vantage points along the river. As they watched the tawny waters, they sensed without being able to express it, some secret relationship between this mighty onward-rushing stream and the Fate that seemed to be carrying them where it would. They renewed their pledges repeatedly, promising to exchange full news chronicles each time a letter could be carried. By relays a messenger might travel as fast as sixty miles in twenty-four hours. . . .

Ripe summer on the Danubian plains, ruby on their vineyards, russet on the unending rolling grain lands. In the villages dotting them, whose thatched roofs were lower than the clustering trees, autumn flowers filled the gardens, and bees hummed under the linden branches. There was as yet more dust than mud on the long road to the north. At this time of year the magical Tatra mountains would glow like opals against the sky; the air would be filled with the resinous scent of pine and fir trees. Had she been starting forth with her mother and Mary and William, Jadwiga would have been all excitement at the prospect of such a journey. But alone, and to what experience? She was brave, she was remembering her father, and Saint Jadwiga and Saint Margaret and listening to the fortifying counsel of priests and teachers. But she kept pathetically close to her loved ones during these last days.

The morning arrived. Jadwiga and Mary, awake long before dawn, threw open the inside wooden shutters and the membrane-covered sash, and then, running back to bed for warmth and closeness, watched for sunrise. It came with October splendor.

They ran again to the window. The air was burnished; one drank it like wine. The shining river and ridges winding eastward and westward, the town of Pest below on the Danube edge of the great valley stretching northward—all were silver in the first light. How they, so soon to be separated, loved every part of this world of beauty which belonged to them together.

The whole hill was astir early. For days, resplendent officials, excited dames of honor, picked soldiers and knights wearing emblazoned surcoats over their armor and carrying hooded falcons on their wrists, had been joyously arriving from Poland to escort their prospective queen to her capital. Others from all parts of Hungary were crowding in on Pest and Buda, either to have just an onlooker's share in the historic event or because they had been fortunate enough to be chosen to accompany King Louis' daughter part or all of the way.

The assembling court for the heavy supply wagons, for oxen and horses and falcons and hounds, was a center of advance activity. The royal commissary was making unusually early preparations for daytime and nighttime comfort in furnishings and food. This was to be a journey whose like the world had not seen. Their great King Louis' daughter was going away to be a queen—theirs the duty of seeing that she lacked nothing on the long welcoming way—perhaps it would be a crowded month before she reached Krakow.

The activity without the place was matched by that within, where young and old pressed for some opportunity to help in getting Jadwiga ready. As they hurried about, Anna, young Elizabeth, and the group of ladies to accompany her, ran frequently to reassure Queen Elizabeth. Fortunately, things to be done so occupied her and Mary and Jadwiga herself, that emotions which might otherwise have overwhelmed them were held in abeyance. They had little time alone. Nicholas Gara, or Scribe John, or the Bishop of Veszprem, or some other family counselor, was repeatedly appearing for orders or to offer advice.

Finally came the call to start. The supply wagons and those carrying the treasure chests filled with rugs and embroideries and much silver and gold and jewels, already rumbled on their way. Pennants unfurled on the early wind. At the head of the forming line floated the Church banner with its embroidered figure of Saint Ladislaus, Hungary's patron saint who would protect them on their way. The swift eastern horses were saddled. Jadwiga's white one had been chosen from hundreds; her saddle was inset with ivory. Yet she was to ride most of the way in the gilded coach. The escort of clergy and nobles and dames and the honored of Hungary's army were assembling. The company might have been setting out from Paris, so many were the costumes and weapons copied from French models. Scarlet vied with green and purple, jewelled collar with gorgeously incrusted scabbard; choristers in white carried branches of trees.

Despite her grief, Jadwiga's youth responded to the beauty of her own white robe and blue velvet mantle embroidered with gold lilies of France. She carried a little travelling altar-piece. It looked like a small book with a silver binding, but when she opened it and set it up, there were seen to be depicted inside it, in ivory of exquisite French workmanship, scenes from the gospels, the flight into Egypt, the raising of Lazarus, the Crucifixion. She would never be separated from this and from her rosary.

Good Cardinal Dimitri of Estergom who had performed the ceremony at Hainburg and had long been her friend and William's, and with him Bishop of John of Csanad and Doctor Radlica, who was now Bishop of Krakow, came to take over their charge. Jadwiga might have succeeded in restraining her tears as she had vowed to, had the group of weeping servants and friends not crowded about her. Pale, and struggling to appear brave, she turned to her adored mother for last reassurances and embraces, then to her only sister and her comrade-lover.

At the last William found few words. He clung to her hand, threw his arm about her, trying to delay, even for a minute, her going. But now Archbishop Dimitri gave the word. One more embrace and Jadwiga was seated in the coach. Silver spurs and stirrups clicked, and with many calls and hand wavings, the cavalcade headed north.

The group on Buda Hill watched until it was no more than a speck on the horizon and finally was blotted out. Even then, William refused to go inside with the others, but remained long on the rampart, his eyes on the north.

He would himself soon be leaving Buda. Vienna was not farther off, perhaps, in miles from Krakow, than Buda was, but it seemed farther, because Jadwiga and he had faced the Polish capital together from here. His father's court would be no quiet place to dream in—troubles with Venice and Switzerland alone meant continuous military preparation. However, they would not succeed in holding him long in Vienna. But even while he was trying to comfort himself with this assertion, he realized that for a whole year yet he would not be his own master.

What a strange journey was the triumphal progress of this young girl. For centuries girls have ridden across the eastern plains, yet as we look backward only one rides as she. Destiny, again, from the multitude selected one to write an imperishable story against the skies. . . .

Fortunately, as the distance from home slowly, steadily, lengthened, Jadwiga's thoughts had little time at their own disposal. The days were bright with changing scenes, and their hours were filled with instruction. At night the cavalcade halted, and there were daytime stops as well at monasteries or chateaux for rest and refreshment, not only for riders, but also for horses. At Dios Györ, the castle her father had so loved, Jadwiga's mind was filled with memories of King Louis and of the days she and William had spent on the surrounding tree and flower covered slopes. Here a holy monk who could walk barefoot on red hot iron, joined the royal procession. The high-walled city of Kassa, too, was familiar—how joyously she and her mother had retreated from it, back along the spring-flooded valley which she had now retraversed!

Beyond Kassa the way soon wound into the wilder Carpathian mountain region, where her eyes were quick to enjoy the changing colors and contours and swift waters of one of the loveliest regions in the world. When she was not following a narrow canyon, looking up through mists of waterfalls, past level upon level of mounting conifers, to the deep blue sky strip above, she was skirting some sapphire lake set in a high meadow carpeted with orchids and tiger lilies and gentians, or climbing a sheer mountain side where dwarf junipers thrust from the rocks, while below her dropped dim canyon depths. Often in honey-scented woods she heard stags calling their love songs to the does. She was glad that both Hungary and Poland had a share in these marvelous mountain lands.

In all towns along the route the queen to be was met by nobles and functionaries of the crown. "Praised be Jesus Christ!" called a new arrival. "Forever and ever, Amen!" rang the reply. "May God bless you seven times daily," said an approaching knight; while another cried, "Glory be to Saint George!" All announced their names, escutcheons, service, and the village by which they entitled themselves. Many knights were shiningly prepared to enter the lists in the tournaments that would accompany the coronation; some of them wore coats of mail made in Milan, than which there were no finer. An English yeoman, in a coat and hood of green, was welcomed warmly. He wore on his breast a silver image of Saint Christopher, patron of field sports, and carried a bow and a quiver filled with peacocks' arrows. All who hoped for favors were ready to embrace the feet of the new queen.

At the frontier Jadwiga was received with much pomp by the great nobles. The frontier! She had felt that there must be some visible line of separation; that the soil of Poland would somehow look different from the soil of Hungary. But except for the welcoming groups she would not have known that she had passed beyond her own loved land. And except for the new Saint. People now wore images of Saint Stanislaus instead of Saint Ladislaus. Jadwiga made the sign of the Cross and prayed for the blessing of Poland's patron saint.

The Slav villages acclaimed her as their magistrates offered her on a carved wooden plate the salt-and-bread pledge of hospitality. Instantly her beauty and girlish grace, her directness, coupled with modesty, won eyes and hearts. She was lovely; strong, yet unassuming; she was good. Her coming meant deliverance from the long nightmare of dissension and suffering. The people could scarcely control their joy.

She made a special halt at Sacz, to visit the shrine

of Princess Kunegunda, who, a Hungarian like herself, had also given up her country for Poland, where because of her holiness she had been named a saint. She prayed fervently for the blessing of Saint Kunegunda. In this age of mystic piety it was not uncommon for noblewomen to end their days in convents; Jadwiga knew their stories. Often on this journey, her royal company had passed bands of dust-covered pilgrims, en route to Wilsnach, near Breslau, a center for the devotion of the Blessed Virgin.

Once again en route, she gave herself up to enjoyment of the streams and the beeches and oaks and firs of the wooded slopes of Galicia. But she was always content to reach a village or a town, which she often found to be a vigorously young one, founded by her Great Uncle, Poland's King Casimir. Casimir had inherited from his father, King Lokietek, a realm for the first time strongly defined, so that he had been able to give rein to his noble impatience for social and economical progress. He had encouraged the free growth of these Polish towns until they were practically self-governing. He had given them defensive walls, better bridges and roads, better courts and protection by law, encouraged their flour and saw mills and trade in general. She visited their churches and delighted in their bright bazaars. Everywhere she saw evidence of Casimir's wise rule and heard accounts of his statesmanlike acts; not unmingled it is true with tales of wild escapades, for he had an exuberant nature prompt to yield to temptations of the senses!

As she pushed forward on the way crowded with interest for her young mind, many more nobles and burghers joined her escort; so many, in fact, that she seemed toward the end to be accompanied by a whole kingdom. A minstrel and his group of singing students had attached themselves and now added their songs to the music of the advance. At the cities of Wieliczka and Bochnia she stopped to visit the famous salt mines whose weirdly beautiful chapels and altars and great halls carved from salt crystal still today dazzle our tourist eyes, and she longed to share their subterranean fairy world with William. The Poles employed Italians to manage these mines and they managed them well. Jadwiga had counted along the way more wagons filled with salt than with hemp and skins and honey. And then at last (she had left Buda over a half month ago) before her stood Krakow, her new home—Krakow, pearl of Poland, set in the glowing autumn hill country. It lay on the left bank of the broad Vistula, its palace-crowned Wawel Hill and the Bishop's Skalka Hill and other eminences lifting above the line of the many-towered city walls. She could see the white eagle of Poland on a red field unfurled above the palace on the royal hill.

She was met outside the great gate—Kazimierz Gate—by a delegation of the clergy and nobles. Advancing joyously came the high clergy with their banners, the chanoines of all the convents, the guilds with their flags and ribbon streamers, and the municipal council in silken robes and silver belts and round velvet bonnets. Strong men bore the city flag on which were embroidered in gold three square towers, the outer ones crowned by the figures of the patron saints, Stanislaus and Wenceslaus, and the middle one by the Polish eagle. The many Krakovians wearing red caps whose folded points sometimes hung down at the side below the waist added brilliant flecks of color to the human tide that surged to meet the daughter of King Louis. Could Elizabeth, anxiously trying to picture the progress, see all banners dip as her child approached? The city presented a gift, symbol of submission and homage, and to the music of trumpets and flutes and the cries of the hilarious crowd, Jadwiga entered the capital.

There she found that all that had passed so far had been only a prelude. Great bells sounded, bonfires flared in the enormous market place and open squares, lanterns illumined the streets. A procession of girls in white, rose garlanded and carrying lighted candles came to meet their girl queen. Groups of singing students wound in and out through the dense throng. She encountered a very delirium of welcome.

This was by no means the expression of mere excitement. Before any formal exchanges—swiftly, mysteriously, one of those profound exchanges so potent in history, occurred. The warm-hearted, full-blooded youth of the nation flowed out to meet the glowing youth of this girl who had come from a great kingdom to remain for life with them. No more absenteeism! She belonged to them—and they loved her!

The rejoicing followed her to the royal Hill, that same walled Wawel Hill, which with its gothic Cathedral and palace, is the glory of Krakow today. There, according to custom, she went first to the Cathedral, the crowning place and burial place of Poland's kings. She knelt below the high altar and the holy relics were brought out and she kissed them, then offered her gifts. When at last she crossed the wide court that separated the Cathedral from the royal chateau, which at this time embraced three houses, she was, despite her vigor, beneath her silk and velvet robes, a very tired young girl.

But she could not give way to youthful weariness now. She was queen of one of the great countries of Europe. Outside, her people were still dancing and singing because she had come to them. The Hungarians who had escorted her were celebrating with them. She was glad that her stone chamber with its vaulted gothic ceiling was no larger, not so large as the neighboring one in which her great Uncle Casimir had died. She would have felt lonelier had it been. She was for the moment alone. Anna was occupied with the chests and with finding her place in this new home. She walked to the stone steps leading up to the narrow alcoved window and two lower opposite window seats. It was not nearly so large a window as that in her mother's room. She swung the casement open. Down below the tops of the great trees of the steeply dropping hill slope she could see her capital. A certain bell was still ringing and its tones held her ear. How smoothly, how easily, the silver notes floated above the city and off towards the east—they seemed to be travelling east, where her mind pictured no barrier. Farther and farther on the blue air these silver notes would travel—if only they could carry southward across the Carpathians and sound above Buda a message to William and Mary and her mother!

CHAPTER X

Jadwiga's New Home

As she stood alone by the little window of her gothic chamber, looking down on her capital, with its far-sweeping wall and moat and many fringing villages, Jadwiga could not see the broad Vistula, but she knew that it flowed by the base of the hill. She was glad it was there—how could one live where there was no river? The Danube was part of her. And she was glad that her palace was on a hill as the others had been at Visegrád and at Buda—not so high nor so beautiful a hill, to be sure—not a crest in looping, spreading ranges—these were farther away from the city—but it was nevertheless a hill. And the province of Galicia in which lay the Grand Duchy of Krakow, was as lovely a rolling land of glens and streams as one could wish to see. Within the capital's walls below lived not only the good Krakow burghers but practically all of the nobility holding state offices. She had already learned that the old rivalry between the first Polish capital, Gnezno, in the province of Great Poland, and Krakow, was not yet buried. There were those who would have rejoiced to see her crowned at more northern Gnezno on Lake Golpo. She was thankful that there was no question of her going farther away. She was sure that she much preferred Krakow.

She turned to examine her deep-walled apartment and its location more closely. Her window looked to the northeast. From another part of the chateau she would be able on clear days to see the glowing peaks of the Carpathian mountains which separated her two countries. Her first impression had been correct; this was a bright room with a corner fire-place to make it comfortable. The walls were painted a warm cinnabar tint. It was longer than wide, and the vaulting ribs of the ceiling were caught at three equally spaced points by graceful bosses. The doorway opposite the window end (all the doorways carried a benediction of beauty) led to an irregular corridor, large enough, perhaps, to serve as a dressing-room, and thence to her Uncle Casimir's large square chamber with its fine hooded fire-place. From this same corridor, ornamented with a frescoed frieze of vines and grape clusters, a secret way led to the formal reception rooms. There seemed to be many hidden passageways and mysterious narrow staircases leading up or down. There were enormous cellars below this first palace floor, which was itself entered from the courtyard by a double flight of steps and a stone platform. It stretched along to the administration offices and kitchens; in fact, the working quarters of the chateau were apparently all on this level, conveniently near. Leaning from a small window, she could see the kitchen court, where a fish vendor in a long kaftan and belt was delivering gleaming fish and slippery eels from a low barrel on his sled.

The apartments of her ladies in waiting were not far from her chamber. To the right of it, a few steps down, was an informal reception hall with a barrel ceiling, and beyond it a spacious doubly vaulted room. Where would William choose to be? In Casimir's large chamber? Probably. Her grandmother, she believed, had occupied this smaller one of her own—that thought was comforting. It was pleasingly furnished; she liked particularly the brightly woven tapestry representing the resurrection, which hung over her low wooden plank bed placed against the right wall. From this bed, with its dimity-covered mattresses and pillows and fine spreads, she would be able to look through the narrow window at morning and evening skies. The hill dropped so swiftly that she would not see the tree tops, but she would know where they were. Many skins and eastern carpets promised protection from the cold floor; the two fur rugs in front of her bed, and another before the prie-dieu next to the bed were white and soft.

A commodious, gaily painted chest of drawers stood at either side of the window, and a heavily carved wardrobe and chairs against the wall opposite her bed. The table in the middle of the room was large enough to hold her embroideries and books and flowers. She would be able to read and embroider at night as well as by day, for there would be plenty of light from the half dozen large brass candle reflectors on the walls each holding three or four candles. Besides, there was an oil lamp on the table.

She could hear a group of ladies in waiting moving about in their apartments nearby; some of them she already knew. They were singing as they worked, and farther away court musicians were vigorously playing Slavic airs. She felt that she was going to like particularly her lady in waiting young Constance of Koniecpolska, who seemed reliable and companionable. She and others would soon be coming to her. But before they came she wanted to look again from her window, again, alone, to try to feel her way toward the city and its citizens who had so marvelously welcomed her.

She had been brought up on its legendary as well as its authentic history. Krakow was surrounded by a web of poetical stories. Under this very Wawel Hill on which she stood, gloomed the cave where once lived the dragon that had exacted a tribute of human victims from the lower village, and from whose hideous grip Krakus, mythical founder of the capital, had delivered the people. There had been centuries of pagan worship. The lovely little chapel outside in the courtyard had been a pagan shrine until the coming of Saint Cyril and Saint Methodius, missionaries of Christ. Then everything had changed. And toward the close of the eleventh century Archbishop Stanislaus had become Poland's patron saint, after a feud between mitre and crown, which had resulted in the murder of the archbishop by the king.

Step by step events had led to the great reign of her uncle. Before him the first Casimir had settled a colony of Benedictines from Liége on this Wawel Hill, and through them religion and the culture of the west had spread, just as they had through the Benedictines whom her father had so encouraged in Hungary. Here in Galicia they had been given a royal castle and lands at Tyniec, about five miles from Krakow, where they developed their rich possessions until they had not less than a hundred villages under their administration. On her journey to Krakow she had sighted from miles away the towers of their abbey which looked proudly down from a cliffhead into the reflecting waters of the Vistula. She would never forget the warmth and splendor of her reception within the abbey's hospitable gates.

The weeks of travel from her own to her new country had been weeks filled with lessons, as one after another of her escort had explained something she had not yet known, or reviewed with her things she had been taught, but which were now, for the first time, intensely real. She had already made her first contacts with the majority of those who were to be counsellors during her minority, which did not mean, however, that they did not still seem strangers.

They talked to her repeatedly of her uncle Casimir's affection for Krakow—for all of his cities, but especially for the fair city of Krakow. Already she had seen that it was beautifully planted; its founders had brought an experienced land surveyor with them who had laid it out and marked off the harmonious lines of the central market place. From this "Ring" with its fine long Clothiers' Hall and Hôtel de Ville and lofty Cathedral of Saint Mary, six wide streets radiated to the six city gates. Casimir had found it a city of wood and left it largely a city of stone, more strongly fortified than it had ever been before and greatly advanced in trade and in culture. He had always welcomed new ideas and methods. In fact, under him the city became so powerful that he was forced several times to discipline it for insubordination.

Jadwiga, trying to get her bearings, had to think back to Casimir. She knew that her grandmother, the vivid gay Queen Regent Elizabeth, had made Wawel court an intellectual center known throughout Europe, yet the whole period between peace-loving Casimir and herself had been in so many ways disastrous to Poland, and she must turn back to him as her guide. She, too, would try to make her capital more beautiful, build churches and schools and parks.

Like her father, Casimir had been a born ruler. He was, strikingly, in his day, a lover of peace, not an idle, but a fecund peace; his reign saw a succession of peace treaties and works of peace. He had given his exhausted country a blessed breathing space of thirty-seven years. Yet, he had, she had been taught, in one instance at least, paid perhaps too great a price for peace, when he had turned over the province of Silesia to the Czech king to win that dangerous neighbor's renunciation of claims to the Polish throne. But he had added to Poland rich Red Ruthenia, and this jewel of her crown she must especially guard.

She was impressed by the kinship between many of her great uncle's aims and those of her father. Casimir had been called the Peasants' King because of his efforts for those usually neglected by monarchs. Not only had he shared the royal corn with them in times of famine, but he had given them protection against oppressive landlords through a codification of laws and a reform in the administration of justice. More than that, he had personally supervised the enforcement of these laws. Above the peasants were the thriving burgher class, then the lesser nobles, and finally the great nobles. The Jews crowded below these groups. To them, as well, Casimir showed a tolerance not practiced by other monarchs, not practiced, indeed, by her father. It was in their attitude toward the burgher class that the father and uncle who were her guides seemed nearest each other. Louis had been, in Hungary, like Casimir in Poland, particularly the friend of men who by their skill and industry were bringing greater wealth to the state, and more comfort to all. She wished, too, to be the friend of her townspeople.

This was the age of the Marian devotion, of the elevation of all women through One. Recently Saint Bridget of Sweden had thrilled the world with her brilliant participation in Church and state affairs. The story of Saint Catherine's dramatic effort at

Rome and sad death there were fresh in her memory. Jadwiga longed with all the intensity of her piety to do herself what Christ and the Church expected of her. It was blessed to remember, so far from home, that though countries and peoples changed, the great Catholic Church remained one. There was her true home.

In Hungary her world had seemed vast enough, but how bewilderingly its boundaries were widening. Now the powerful Germans were just to the west of her; Königsberg and Marienburg, headquarters of the Knights of the Cross not far to the north. She and William knew well the record of the knights as glorious hunters of pagans. But from henceforth she would have to hold her mind to a different view of them. Their name spelled terror to Poland; their bloodhounds were unleashed on her border. No subject of hers on going to bed near that border could be sure that he would not awake beneath a flaming roof. And pagan Lithuania, which still resisted all the evangelizing zeal of the Christian world, was her next door neighbor. To the east lay Moscovy—beyond it ranged the Golden Horde—her mind was lost when it tried to grapple with the problems these proximities implied.

She was, of course, not yet actually to rule, though she had been painstakingly instructed in the theory of the Polish state. A progressive among mediæval European countries, it was moving in the direction of an elective monarchy and parliamentary government.

It had an advisory council of the crown and a national diet in which theoretically all the people, but actually only the nobility and clergy, were represented; although since the beginning of this year delegates from the towns were allowed to sit with nobles and clergy in the royal council. All of this, however, did not mean that the great provinces were yet committed to a strongly centralized government; for each was still jealous of its sovereignty.

During the disastrous interregnum which her coming had ended, independent rivalries of provincial heads had reduced the land to almost hopeless disunion. Alone the frequent church synods, which represented the whole of Poland, had seemed to keep alive the idea of national solidarity. For the moment, the nobles of the province of small Poland, who were her ardent supporters, were the dominant power in the land. She was to be under their tutelage, and directly under that of Castellan Dobieslaw, military commander of Krakow and mayor of the royal chateau. Dobieslaw was broad-shouldered, bearded, powerful, with penetrating eyes which looked out from under dark brows. What would he be like as guardian? Fortunately, there was at least one official for whom she would have a kind of family feeling; the assistant treasurer, old Dimitri of Goray who had served under both her uncle and her father.

Everything had been properly looked after—she was familiar with court machinery—her dames of honor and maidens in waiting were ready to serve her.

The Duchess of Mazovia, sister of the Piast claimant of the crown, Ziemowit, who had attempted to kidnap her, would be one of the most influential women of her entourage! Anna would never be far from this chamber. Her dear, cheering Elizabeth and others who had accompanied her to her new home lived down in the city at the foot of the hill. Yet in reality she was alone. All her youth had responded to the breath-taking scenes of which she had been the central figure. But now the tide of excitement and exaltation receded and left a loneliness which would have been unendurable but for the thought that William would soon arrive to share this too vast, too complex, world with her. She leaned on that belief.

Anna came shortly. Then Elizabeth, her brown hair rippling rather untidily about her low, broad forehead, and her eyes shining with excitement over the importance of her new duties and privileges. With her was Constance, fairer and taller, and wearing a flat fluted headdress of thin muslin. One could read in the decision of her step and erectness of her bearing that she was clear-minded and executive. She was still unmarried, while Elizabeth's husband, Spytko, lord of Meltzyn castle, was one of the most intrepid and loved knights in the whole kingdom. The women spent several busy hours with their young queen arranging quarters and possessions. And during supper they planned for the morrow. Archbishop Dimitri and other Buda friends came in to see how she was getting settled, and with blessing and good-wishing to bid her good-night. And then again she was alone, her mind busy with those inner adjustments hidden from others.

Brave, pathetic little figure in the northern gothic chamber, trying to think it out! Unconsciously, she was opening doors to all the teachings and influences of her extraordinarily crowded young years—they were now to prove their worth. Casimir through his choice of Louis as successor, had brought disaster to Poland. Now here was Louis' daughter. She turned from the window and set up the little silver altarpiece on the low oak stand beside her bed. After meditations and prayers, she tried to sleep. And as spring rains fill the lily's chalice, so thoughts of William filled her heart.

CHAPTER XI

Jadwiga Twice Crowned

THE Polish white eagle floated gaily high above Wawel chateau. During this very week of her arrival, on October 15, 1384—her name day—Jadwiga was to be crowned. Anna had not left her room during the night. Constance and the others were up at dawn; never before had there been so beautiful a queen to attend. She herself had waked long before they had, her thoughts not on the crown, but on Buda. Brightly, indeed, would this day have dawned could but the three she loved have shared it! As her fingers slipped over her rosary beads, she lifted her thoughts to her father—surely he was looking down on her. How often he had pictured to her her coronation, not here in Wawel Cathedral, but in Hungary's coronation Cathedral at Székes Fehérvár. What was he thinking of the changes Fate had ordained since he left them? She prayed for his blessing as she knelt before the crucifix.

Then came the hour for which her already devoted dames and maidens of honor impatiently waited. Amidst exclamations of admiration, and excitement which they could scarcely control, they spread on the bed her dawn-white robe and her mantle of crimson velvet and set the high-backed, square-toed sandals of red velvet embroidered with crosses of gold before it. They made suggestions about the myriad details of the royal toilet, eager, each, to have a hand in arranging her wondrous hair and the veil of finest gauze that would be folded back from her forehead. Anna, despite her superfluous pounds, seemed to be in all parts of the room at once. Jadwiga's full-blooded youth responded more and more freely to this encircling enthusiasm. Indeed, when a little later in the morning, Archbishop Bodzanta with the three heads of administration—the commander of the castle, Dobieslaw; the palatin, representing the whole palatinate; and the governor, who administered the properties of the king and the state, along with other important nobles and ecclesiastics, arrived for a preliminary service in the chateau, she seemed to them the very incarnation of youth's buoyancy and loveliness. They were strangely moved by a certain fine valiancy in her bearing.

Jadwiga felt that this preparatory ceremony would be more intimately real and impressive than the elaborate ritual to follow. For in the Cathedral she would be too overcome by emotions stirred by the presence of the acclaiming company and by the memories of Poland's past which already filled this loved Pantheon built in her century, to be able to realize fully what was taking place. Her father had been crowned before the high altar. Her uncle Casimir with other kings and their queens lay in the crypt below it. Each of the sacred objects in the treasury; the carved crystal chalices, the white mitre of Saint Stanislaus adorned by its double cross of blue, the silver reliquary filled with earth from the Holy Sepulcher, which had been presented to Saint Jadwiga, for whom she was named—these things would add their suggestions of piety and devotion. So it was that she felt that in this earlier hour she was experiencing more clearly than she could later, her own part in the tremendous day.

After the apartment had been sprinkled with holy water, all knelt, and in the solemn quietness prayers were read.

While this ceremony was in progress inside the palace, the scene outside was tumultuous. Music of kettledrums and trumpets filled the air. From the courtyard, on past the Cathedral to the bastions, and down the curving hill road to the lower wall, surged the crowds that had been fortunate enough to pass the gate. Each lay or ecclesiastical representative of a province or city, each ambassador and princely foreign guest was accompanied by his suite. Every few minutes the gathered thousands welcomed with a shout some belated company—a group of knights fresh from a border encounter—brothers come from a far-distant monastery. When, finally, the archbishop, castellan, governor, and the others escorted Jadwiga, whose spreading crimson mantle was upborne by pages, from the chateau portal down the steps to the courtyard, a wave of intensest emotion swept over the multitude. Eyes of young and old kindled and grew misty, hearts beat faster at sight of her—here was glowing youth whose feet had been forced from the carefree path of youth into the road which wise maturity rarely travelled successfully. But now as she walked, preceded by palatins carrying the royal scepter and coronation sword, protected by a glittering canopy held by high dignitaries, and followed by the abbesses and prioresses of convents and a crowd of courtiers carrying lighted candles, her future appeared all roseate.

At the church portal trumpeters with silver horns, stationed at either side of the wide-swung iron doors of King Casimir, heralded the approach of the procession. Wawel Cathedral had not witnessed a more splendid scene. Its three naves and many chapels were hung with tapestries and banners. The gloom was starred by a thousand candle flames and shot by the wincing gleam of gold and silver. Besides Archbishop Bodzanta and John, Bishop of Krakow, Dimitri of Estergom who had betrothed Jadwiga at Hainburg and had buried her father and crowned her sister Mary, and other Hungarian prelates who had escorted their princess to Poland, were to officiate at the altar.

In the chapel at the right of the choir, King Louis' daughter was robed in the traditional alb, tunic, and dalmatique, and while the scepter and sword were laid upon the altar, she advanced through a glittering avenue of nobles toward the throne erected in the middle of the nave, near the tomb of Saint Stanislaus. There her suite halted and the mass began. Crystalline bells sounded, the chalice was lifted, from swinging censors incense rose in clouds about the candle flames, organ-thunder sounded through the packed naves. Before the Gospel, Jadwiga approached the altar to hear the age-old question, winged with inextinguishable faith and hope—"Would she promise to respect all the rights, the liberties, and privileges of the people?" All heard her clear, firm "Yes." And she meant to keep that promise, dear child, as she understood it. She wanted people to be happy and free—to have homes and families and to be able to stay with them. She knelt to receive the unction. Then she placed before the altar her offering of bread and wine in a golden receptacle, while, following her example, each noble offered his. And as candles were lifted and music and the happy cries of children and men and women flooded the church, and her whole being was swept by an answering emotion, she took her place on the throne.

She was crowned king, not queen; but since her mother had neglected to return the king's crown which her father had taken to Hungary, the beautiful but heavy gold one with its pendant ribbons now taken from the altar to the throne had been hurriedly made in Krakow for the occasion. Two dignitaries held it over her head during the remainder of the ceremony. At its close, the jubilant cortège returned across the courtyard to the chateau, where a state banquet, over which their girl queen presided, ended the day.

Later, an image of her as she appeared at this coronation was stamped on one of the seals which she attached to her documents, one of the most elaborate seals of her century. Executed in wax, and ornamented with long green and red ribbons, it pictures her on the gothic throne of the Cathedral. In the wings at either side are angels, and in the two wings still beyond, arms of the most important Polish princely houses.

The ceremony was not yet complete, for in all that had passed so far the Krakow burghers had had no part. The following day, again royally robed and attended, Jadwiga went from Wawel Hall down to the city. It was a beautiful descent. She rode in the gilded state carriage, followed by her suite, from her chateau across the wide-spreading courtyard and under the triple gateway, out past the Cathedral and Benedictine cloister and school for the clergy, past the Thieves' Tower, to the splendid terrace which commanded a view over valley and hills to the horizon, Southward, beyond the Carpathians lay Hungary—Buda and her mother and Mary!

The road dropped down from the terrace along the southern hill face, to the river level. Here the hillside was so steep that the earth above and below had to be held by retaining walls. But the road itself was pleasantly graduated. All round the base of the hill ran the protecting moat and wall. And everywhere were beautiful trees and shrubs, still holding, on this seventeenth of October, their gold and russet of autumn.

The driver held in his six horses and as the carriage rumbled slowly down, Jadwiga got a good view of the Skałka, that smaller Bishop's Hill, embraced forkwise by the river, on which Archbishop Stanislaus had been murdered by King Boleslas the Bold. The fortified island village which her uncle named after himself, Casimirtown, stood conspicuously at her right. There he had tried unsuccessfully to establish a university. Several other villages clustered near the capital; Casimir had often favored one or another of them in order to punish Krakow for some insubordination. Her eyes could follow for some distance the moat and many-towered wall of the waiting city.

The glittering carriage rolled out through the gateway, and past the buildings clustered near the Wawel entrance—past the fortress church of Saint Andrew, with its two octagonal towers. This church, with its great loft over the side aisle, capable of holding 150 persons, had more than once, the young queen knew, served as a refuge for kings and princes in time of trouble. Casimir's father, King Lokietek, after hiding there, had escaped over its walls. A little farther along she passed near the hospitable Franciscan monastery, but without divining the part it was soon to play in her life.

Then, still following Castle street, the procession came in a few minutes to the heart of the old town. For this chief city of the Grand Duchy of Krakow was indeed old—in the ninth century it had been a bishop's seat. Its palpitating center was the immense market place, one of the most extraordinary in Europe, flanked by palaces of the nobility and wealthy burghers. Today all were gay with banners and brilliant hangings. As were the long central Clothiers' Hall, the Hotel de Ville near one end of the square, and the quaint little church of Saint Adalbert at the other end, marking the place where Adalbert preached on his way to Prussia and a martyr's death. At the north side of the square beautiful Saint Mary's Cathedral dominated the scene.

A great shout of welcome rose from the immense concourse of men and women as Jadwiga approached along the route barred off for the royal procession. Today burghers were welcoming their queen, coming to be the second time crowned and sceptered and to sit upon the throne they had erected before their City Hall. About it were grouped the mayor, accompanied by liveried archers armed with swords, the city councillors, judges, and other officials—forty in number.

When at last the queen sat enthroned under the blue sky, with the October sunlight gilding her crown and firing the bannered façades of the flanking palaces, there arose another great shout. Now she solemnly confirmed the rights and privileges of the city, and received the vows of its citizens.

Here she was at last face to face with her subjects, who were ready to love her, and in no anemic way. In her beautiful Slavic capital the tide of vitality ran high. The people were intense in their loyalties and their mystical adorations, as they were, indeed, in their immoralities. These, however, did not prevent them from trooping into the churches, into Saint John's and Saint Florian's, Saint Nicholas' and the others, as dutifully as children.

This multitude acclaiming her today represented a very large population, possibly nearing half a million, which had seemed scarcely diminished when just before her time twenty thousand had died of plague. It was a very mixed population, including rich Tatars, money-lending Jews, Armenians, and several other large foreign groups. Great numbers had come from less tolerant lands to Casimir's friendly capital. The fact that he, himself a Catholic, had wisely instructed a Byzantine patriarch to found bishoprics under the orthodox church in Poland's Russian dominions, had profoundly impressed the outside world.

The Krakovians were of a joyously materialistic disposition. They ate much and danced long and fought hard. The brilliant costumes of the men scandalized more serious communities. Indeed, the feasts of wealthy merchants which often rivalled those of the Wawel itself, had once been the cause of a sumptuary law which prohibited more than five courses and more than thirty dishes at wedding banquets. Jesters, too, were limited to eight. And the bride could receive no gifts of silk clothing!

Many trades flourished. Trade was the strength of the city as the guilds were of trade. Jadwiga's father had from the first granted special favors to the residential capital, opening all the commercial routes to it. The powerful guilds had established themselves one after another in towers built into the far-circling city walls, where they added to their normal duties those of defense. They owned some thirty towers. And all were represented here at this coronation; lace makers, tanners, book-binders, rope makers, masons, brewers, butchers, bellows makers, joiners, silversmiths—a host of the cleverest artificers and tradesmen of the continent swelled the crowd.

As Jadwiga sat, crowned and sceptered, on the throne before the City Hall, cutting across her subjects' joyous acceptance of their little queen shot the question, Who will sit beside her? For most of them wanted a king—a strong king—who would protect them against the more powerful nobles of their own country, and the entire country against the dreaded invasions of the Order of Teutonic Knights and the Lithuanians. They were not thinking of the fourteen-year-old prince of Austria!

CHAPTER XII

The Girl Queen

THREE days after she had been crowned the second time before the City Hall, Queen Jadwiga was signing documents—first documents, seemingly of no especial importance, but today how venerated! Historians like to point out that the initial act of her reign confirmed the right of a man of the middle class, one Sidel, to certain lands he had bought. The people looked on this as a sign that their beautiful girl queen would prove herself kin of their great Casimir.

The crown was on her head, the scepter in her hand. She knew there could be no hope of dropping them and running back to Buda now! To be sure, at times in the night she dreamed desperately of doing just that. Messages were infrequent, letters took so long to come and go. What had been happening at Visegrád this week? What was going on in Scribe John's bookshop at Buda? Had her mother perhaps repeated for the young people of the court the excursion to Saint Margaret's Island? Or was there no opportunity for diversion during these days which reports said were increasingly harassing to the queen regent? If she could return but for a week! For an hour! Thus she questioned and battled. However, on the whole her will held her, and her natural resiliency kept her vigorous and eager. She must live up to what her father and heaven expected of her. And always the Blessed Virgin and saints would help her.

Many state matters demanded early action. Those who had done most to help the house of Anjou to the throne must be rewarded, and those who had suffered losses during the civil war must be compensated. Among other promises given during her journey from Buda to Krakow, was that of a gift to the salt mine city of Bochnia, and Jadwiga did not delay to keep her promise. She sent Bochnia money to found a Dominican convent and a church. Thus in her beginning month as queen she began those works of piety which were to follow one after the other throughout her reign.

Her first attention, however, must be given to her own capital city, spreading below Wawel Hill. There had always been rivalry between the royal hill and the town; the struggle for dominance had made their mutual history one of conflict and reconciliation. The era of privileges following the granting of the Krakow charter in 1257, had bred a lusty courage. German merchants, descended from those who came to rebuild the capital, after the Mongolian invasion of 1241 had destroyed practically everything but the Wawel buildings and Saint Andrew's Church, were rich and powerful. They enjoyed the benefits of the Madgeburg municipal law introduced by way of Breslau, and treasured its advantages as symbolizing their independence. At times wealthy burgher leaders gave tournaments and banquets to foreign ambassadors and other princely visitors at court which threatened to eclipse those of the Wawel itself. Jadwiga's uncle, King Casimir, had had a particularly tempestuous experience with these unruly subjects, but finally, after disciplining them in various ways, Casimir had in a gesture of forgiveness made one of them his royal counselor, a post hitherto awarded only to a knight. And after agreeing that the city should have the revenues from the public scales, and small gold and silver smelting works, and house rents, he made other adjustments and re-assumed working relations with it.

As Jadwiga began her rule, conditions were promising. Her father, King Louis, had always treated Krakovians generously and they expected equal kindness from his daughter. She spoke German, which made her seem not a stranger to the controlling German group. German was the language of business; though within the city walls was a jargon of tongues. The large Italian element, too, felt that because of her father she would be sympathetic toward them. Italians were everywhere. One directed the mint, another the Bochnia salt mines from which the crown drew vital revenues; they worked in gold and silver, made hair ornaments, decorated hats and helmets with ostrich and heron's feathers. Then her own Hungarian group had received her with unbounded enthusiasm; they were certain of her favor.

How picturesque, the multi-colored activity of the trade organizations inhabiting the bannered towers of the guilds! They poured their useful wares and luxuries into the yearly trade market, and sent them to the fairs at Gnezno and Poznan, Lublin, and Lvov. Jadwiga's success would depend on the prosperity of these guilds. Great north-south and east-west trade routes converged upon them and then spread away again. She had followed one of them in coming to her new home—there were, indeed, four roads to Hungary. Ever northward along the Buda-Kassa-Sandec-Krakow line rolled wagons heavily freighted with copper, lead, iron, oil. While others returned to Hungary and the south with salt and furs, stuffs from Krakow and Silesia, and yet more cloth, and tin and silver and wax and paper and amber from Germany and England. Or they might bear fruit and wines and fish arrived via Danzig from Flanders, or perhaps manuscripts and paintings and tapestries. Polish merchants competing for foreign trade used constantly the Vistula River and the land route over Thorn to the coast. The stream was dark with barges piled high with wood, worked and unworked. Once traders arrived at the Baltic, they could reach such great exchange centers as Bruges and Wisby and London easily by boat. It was not difficult to understand why in this world men struggled for control of the Baltic. Crossing these north-south lines ran the road to eastern Lvov, city of the Lion, and farther north the one over Lublin to Belz or Wladimir, whence all

Lithuania and Russia lay open. More than the usual perils of trade routes lurked on such roads, the whitening bones of many an intrepid adventurer marked their bandit-infested courses.

The ultimate objectives of many caravans which stopped at Krakow were the Order's wealthy strongholds at Marienburg and Königsberg. Indeed, the royal secretaries were kept busy writing replies to the knights' complaints of Krakow's obstruction of their trade through customs duties and detentions of one sort or another.

Jadwiga was always eager to hear descriptions of Bruges, romantically beautiful city of Flanders, and of nearer Danzig, the Venice of the Baltic, whose enormous warehouses and merchant palaces with gilded painted facades and wide stone street terraces and balustrades made it a city of splendor and dream. She had long greatly desired to visit Danzig. Could she, now queen?

From Krakow a road led also to Silesia—to Breslau, her commercial rival. This was inevitably a dangerous road. And from there, turning southward, reached Prague, where Krakow merchants were allowed to trade by a special privilege granted only a half dozen years before Jadwiga's coronation. Following this agreement the Krakow mint had begun to issue money like that of Prague, with the groschen as the small coin. Jadwiga remembered that her father had paid much attention to the designs of his coins, and she hoped to make those of her own reign beautiful.

Each day brought some new interest or knowledge which helped to outline the path she wished to follow. For although the will of the most powerful men of the kingdom focused upon her, Queen Jadwiga's own will was by no means neutralized. Blood of the Piasts and the Anjous flowed in her veins. Controlling powers might shape the frame-work of her days, but within it, young as she was, she found opportunities to initiate and direct.

She seemed rapidly growing to the stature of queen. She had already caught the popular fancy so completely that her people saw her not merely as a young girl set above them on the throne, but as a being exalted in character and wisdom. They remarked how often and how long she was on her knees in the royal chapel seeking counsel and support in prayer. The royal passageway connecting the chateau with the Cathedral knew her well.

It seemed strange to have much older women looking to her for leadership. Yet, after all, she was their queen, and with her investment, age had somehow seemed to drop its mantle on her young shoulders. But while she led, she followed, too, depending most for advice and support on such experienced persons as the wives of the governors of her provinces. Among them one of her especial friends was dark-haired, blue-eyed, smiling Katherine, wife of the governor of eastern Lvov, which faced the great Ukraine country.

But the one to whom she turned oftenest in her

need for friendship—alone as she was, despite the surrounding crowds—was the companion of her childhood, the Hungarian Elizabeth. Her brilliant husband, Spytko, governor of Krakow, was as young in spirit as his wife, so that in this couple the queen found friends sharing her own interests and enthusiasms. Any wife of Spytko would have been near to her, but there was vastly more in the relationship between herself and Elizabeth. From the long chain of their common experience vibrated harmonies of deepest understanding.

Spytko and Elizabeth were not wealthy, but they belonged to the most cultivated Polish group of the capital and whenever they came to Wawel Chateau, these influential, happy people brought to their queen new thoughts and contacts with life outside the court. She was warmly interested in their little family: the first daughter had been named for her sister Catherine, who died before the Hainburg betrothal and the second, Jadwiga, for herself. The queen could not, after all, live on her ideals; occupation with her duties to state and Church could not completely fill her days. More and more she depended on those sweet hours, when forgetting that they were queen and governor's wife, she and Elizabeth were in thought again together at Visegrád or Buda with her mother and Mary and William. Often she felt that without Elizabeth, for whom all these memories were dear and familiar, without this friend to whom she could pour out her heart, she could not have borne her separation.

Sometimes they had the gayest of hours, play hours, that passed like minutes. "Do you remember the little duck swimming in the pond on Visegrád Meadow?" Elizabeth laughed. "What did we say about it?" And Jadwiga, whose voice was rich and vibrant, sang,

> "Little duck is bathing
> In a big black pond.
> He prepares to go to his mother.
> He will be off to Poland."

And, remembering, continued:

> "In the green forest, on the greensward, a bird is walking.
> What kind of a bird?
> It has blue feet and golden feathers, it walks beautifully.
>
> "Wait, thou bird, wait!
> If the Lord has ordered it so,
> Thou shalt be mine."

Elizabeth would match such snatches with her own favorites until the time came for her to go down again to the city.

The queen, young as she was, began early to try to improve the manners and tone of her court. She was quick to encourage good conduct. Following her democratic inclination, she added to her circle certain daughters of burghers, choosing them for their merit. In the beginning there was some grumbling over the rigor of her standards, but love and admiration for her won. Nor did her seriousness of purpose banish gaiety; her own healthy enjoyment of amusements and love of laughter encouraged an atmosphere of joyousness. Since, for her, music was a necessity, it was fortunate that the Poles were as passionately fond of it as the Hungarians themselves—not less than twenty-eight instruments were known to them, the most popular being the trumpet and flute. To a Pole no emotion seemed to have fully flowered until it had found expression in music. Chopin and Paderewski had already begun to be born!

The music-loving queen kept a large court orchestra busy. In the evening, after the many chapel services were over, one after another of her maidens, flower-crowned and lute in hand, would take her place on the bench pulled out into the middle of the chamber, and entertain her with worldly songs. Jadwiga, always generous in praise, often drew the blushing young girl to her, and perhaps teasingly embarrassed her further—"But where rides the knight without peer who fires these cheeks and kindles these notes?"

Yes, healthy gaiety was the witness of a sound court, but not idleness. There was more to be done than arrange the hair and coax the complexion, although some women had as many as three hundred pots of creams and perfumes. With so many chalices to cover and altars to ornament, needles must fly.

Jadwiga interested herself in the decoration not only of the altar of the royal chapel but in embellishing the high altar of the Cathedral and those of increasingly numerous other churches. As soon as she arrived she had begun to embroider cloths and vestments and to encourage the women of her court to do similar work. In this initial year, her own efforts were concentrated chiefly on a magnificent silk rationale—today a treasure in Wawel Cathedral—a sacred vestment a little like the vertical ribbons on the Roman tunic. Using gold threads twice twisted, she embroidered on the white silk in seed pearls the cross and the symbol of the Anjous. A pious monk has since counted the seed pearls she used—42,000 of them!

As on Visegrád Hill, hospitality on Wawel Hill was unstinted. The chateau was a favorite objective, not only for neighbor rulers but for cultivated and romantically-minded travellers from all over Europe. Casimir, and later, Jadwiga's pleasure-loving grandmother, Elizabeth, had swung its doors wide open, and the little queen kept them so. Life here, as in Hungary and elsewhere, was lived in great crowds. If Jadwiga herself went away to visit, she might be accompanied by as many as two or three thousand knights. Visitors were entertained with magnificent banquets and spectacles. The guest who came for dinner at two o'clock was apt to stay on for supper. So the palace housekeeping was a formidable business. Fortunately, the old accounts are still preserved, and as we hold them in our hands and turn their mellow pages on which the neat notations seem as clear as on the day they were set down, Jadwiga and her court are very near. Five hundred chickens were cooked in one day, we read; there were green peas out of season, gilded cakes, and quantities of hydromel, a drink made from the honey of the abundant hives. Her own favorite dish was (as should it not be for a girl?) a delicious cake whose base was pounded almonds.

But though Jadwiga seemed constantly to be entertaining guests, presiding over banquets and tournaments, receiving some foreign ambassador or papal envoy, or sitting with the royal council, she was also doing much hard work of another kind. Daily she was going to school to Church and state. The council of the crown saw to the latter lessons; the priests directed those of the Church. All found at once that they had in her an unusual mind to deal with—keen, intuitive, and at the same time, logical. And, for her age, it was astonishingly furnished. She surprised her new directors with her knowledge of history and economics. They were especially impressed to find this young girl already so accomplished a theologian, delighting in the sermons of the fathers and the lives of the saints. The fearless deeds and flaming speeches of Saint Bridget of Sweden and Saint Catherine of Siena thrilled her; she was later to have certain of their utterances translated into Polish so that her people could follow them at first hand.

The good tidings of her concern for her least subject, of her tender-heartedness, ran across the whole country. Not a day but some sufferer appealed to her charity, and never in vain. She was not content even in these early months merely to endow altars and hospitals; she longed to give direct personal service. Stories show her talking with the aged, reaching out her hand to the poor, lifting the sick child. Pity welled from her lonely heart. No one worked harder than the girl queen. For rest after an especially full relief program, or a tiring council meeting, she used often to slip outside to the garden where, as she sat under one of its great trees, among the birds and flowers, her thoughts winged to Buda.

CHAPTER XIII

A Suitor From the North

As the first year of Queen Jadwiga's reign advanced and 1385 was under way, more insistent was her cry, when will William be allowed to come? She knew that under the terms of her accession she could marry only with the Poles' consent. But when they exacted that promise they knew, as all knew, the sacred character of her "false marriage" with William. By most holy agreement the true marriage would follow after he came of age. He was now fifteen—was he coming? Even as she asked the question, she sensed the network of powerful forces that were holding her lover from her. The road between Vienna and Krakow was no open road. The Poles, the Pope, the Emperor, the Order, her mother—how many watched and sought to control it?

Then suddenly she was all alarm. Her own problem, which was Poland's too, reached a crisis. Promoters of Duke Ziemowit's candidacy for the crown had not ceased working, though their efforts seemed to be swallowed up in controversy. Now there was open talk—unbelievable though it seemed—of the dreaded Jagiello, ruler of pagan Lithuania. Of Jagiello, scourge of Poland, that very "hairy barbarian" whom the poet

Suchenwirt had pictured as she and William had listened shiveringly! She saw with consternation the eyes of the nation turning with hope to the northeast. The Polish nobles were carrying on incredible negotiations with Jagiello, whose capital, Vilno, was a little farther northeast of Krakow than Buda was south of it. Not only would he, if he became King of Poland, unite the vast Lithuanian territories with hers, restore her lost lands, release Polish prisoners of both sexes, and with her defend the united countries against the aggressions of the Order of Teutonic Knights—there was a pledge that meant life—but he would, as he came, embrace Christianity and bring his whole people with him into the Catholic fold!

Here was an amazing offer—none like it was to be found in the annals of Europe. For Lithuania too, it meant tremendous things; a bulwark against Germanism, the Christian religion, admission into the family of Western Europe. But could the offer be genuine? Poland seethed with excitement. Had that hour of which all Christendom dreamed incredibly arrived? Was the prize for which her father and Duke Albert had striven with sword and fire at last within reach? And without stain of war? Religious deeps in her were swept by a great tide. But why, oh why, should fulfillment be possible only by way of her throne? By way of her heart?

The offer must be genuine, for here were Skirgiello and Boris, Jagiello's brothers, and Hanko, the governor of Vilno, and others sent as harbingers already arrived in Krakow. These were not pagans but men baptized in the Greek Orthodox Church. Moreover, Boris, who had lived long in Germany, had been baptized a western Christian. All brought magnificent gifts for the queen and for the Polish nobles. They must be received with honor, and Jadwiga must preside over the assembly. The credulous shivered to know Skirgiello in their midst. Fantastic rumors of his drunkenness and inhuman delight in sawing the bodies of those he had killed into pieces that he might exercise his primitive surgical skill in putting them again together, had long run over the land.

On the eighteenth day of January Wawel courtyard echoed with the clanking of metal and the neighing of horses as leaders of Church and state gathered to welcome this most important mission that had ever crossed the Polish frontier. Conspicuous among them were the familiar figures of Archbishop Bodzanta, Castellan Dobieslaw, Knight Jasko, and the old treasurer, Dimitri of Goray. When the court was assembled and the girl queen in her state robes took her place on the throne, Europe could not have elsewhere matched the scene. Many hearts were wrung with sympathy for her, but some force of Fate seemed to be carrying them all where it would; no girl's love, even though it was a queen's love, could stop it. Anxious eyes were fixed on the door through which the men of the north would enter. When they appeared, Skirgiello at their head, long-haired, bearded, clad in sable and wearing a magnificently jewelled chain and belt, a horn-sheathed knife and a short travelling sword, it was as if a strong wind had swept into the room. An excited murmur shook the company.

There was no evidence of her inward trembling as Jadwiga, with great dignity, received these powerful strangers from a half-mythical land and listened to Skirgiello's address in which, in a voice charged with confident ardor, he set forth the terms of the proposed union. His close-set blue eyes kindled as he pictured the vast territories that Lithuania would add to Poland, the power of this double kingdom to retrieve former losses and to stand against future ones. And then, with mounting emotion, he showed Jagiello coming, not to the throne alone, but into the great family of the western church, bringing with him the entire Lithuanian people.

Jadwiga listened desperately. Had she never loved William she would yet have felt only horror at the thought of marrying a pagan, even though he were a converted one. She knew well that these words would ring the length of the Vistula and the Tisza. They would fall on ears that had so long listened for the word of truce from the north. For a moment all seemed lost, and she cried to a priest standing near, "You who were a witness at Hainburg, can you stand silent now?" But she quickly recovered herself and responded to the discourse with simplicity and courage. There could be but one reply: she was sacredly promised to William of Austria. Moreover, her mother had always been her guide; they must present their proposal to Queen Elizabeth. The last word that had come from Buda had been favorable to William—poor Jadwiga, she still trusted her mother to save her!

So the assembly ended. It was decided that Boris and Hanko with others would proceed to Buda while Skirgiello would wait in Krakow. In Hungary, they would repeat their offer before the queen regent and Mary. Anna, yearning over her queen, over her little girl, tried to hide her tormenting fears. She knew too much to be able to look with hope toward Hungary.

Elizabeth welcomed the mission amiably, though she carefully concealed her inner satisfaction over what she felt, now, at last, meant victory in her ten years' struggle against Austria. Nor did she reveal the relief with which she heard Jagiello's offer to pay William's father the 200,000 florins due him. Nor her intense interest in the religious aspect of this amazing proposal. Boris, after repeating Skirgiello's address delivered in Krakow, spoke for the delegation. "Many Emperors, Kings and Princes," he said, "have sought an alliance with Jagiello, but God postponed this goal for you!" When he closed his eloquent address with the words, "The union we propose to you is a union for the glory of God, the profit of souls and the security of kingdoms," he knew from the faces of his listeners that he had stirred in them profound emotion. However, Elizabeth was too involved in methods of duplicity to act swiftly or directly. And fear of

Austria still stayed her hand. So she said neither no nor yes, but followed discussion with discussion, negotiation with negotiation, until the talking seemed interminable. She tried to commit herself no further than, "We will do our best for the Christian faith, for Poland, and Jadwiga." Her child waiting in Krakow was almost breaking under the strain of the delay. Then, in the end, the queen mother gave her consent to Jagiello's proposal, and Jadwiga's case seemed indeed lost. She added, however, the stipulation that the final decision must rest with the Poles and their queen. That gave her still a chance, perhaps, to save Jadwiga from the suffering which, with a tightening of her heartstrings, she saw looming darkly before her child.

The envoys, confident now of victory, hurried back to Krakow, accompanied by two Hungarians who were to go farther to talk directly with Jagiello. In the capital, the nobles of small Poland hastily convoked a diet. Few from the province of Great Poland took part, because of their loyalty to Duke Ziemowit's cause. This assembly paid no attention to the vital reservation, and hastened to proclaim the project of the marriage with enthusiasm. Jadwiga seemed forgotten. Messengers were dispatched to Vilno to report the decision.

A Magyar delegation now joined the embassy that returned joyfully to Lithuania; for the Hungarians saw in the proposed union protection for their grain fields and vineyards. But above all satisfaction over the material ends visioned, was a universal emotion kindled by the thought that a whole people was to be brought to Christ. By the Treaty of Krewo in 1385, the Poles registered their arrangements with Jagiello.

There was a vastly different emotion in Marienburg and Königsberg, where the Teutonic Order was filled with righteous rage and at once prepared to punish the infidel for his impious plan to convert himself! For in these Knights, once again, the rescuer had become a greater peril than the original enemy. In 1230 when a Polish Duke of Mazovia had appealed to them for protection against his Lithuanian neighbors, they had responded with zeal and called on Christian Europe to aid them in conquering and converting the heathen. But they had not succeeded in converting the Lithuanians, although they had wrested from both Lithuania and Poland valuable lands. How much longer could they continue to draw support from Christian countries, once the glamor of financing a crusade against the last heathen people in western Europe had passed? How continue to add to the lands of the temporal state they aspired to maintain if they could no longer advance under the all-covering white cloak of Order? There was no rejoicing in Marienburg, when the news was carried to the grim citadel of the Order beside the Nogat.

For the will of a girl, pitted as it was against the combined will of Church and state, defeat seemed certain. Yet Jadwiga fought for her love with all the courage of her youth—Oh, when would William arrive? The council of the crown had yet no conception of the measure of her strength and bravery. They were to learn much. They reminded her in vain that Poland had once before allied itself with Lithuania against their common foe when her uncle Casimir had married the daughter of Jagiello's grandfather, Gedymin. All to no avail they represented the thirty-eight-year old suitor as very different from the popular conception of him; as, in fact, a desirable mate for her. Nor did they succeed in convincing her that he was innocent of instigating the murder of his aged uncle Kiejstut, the crime with which Europe rang in the year of her father's death. No vivid picturing of the door to a new era for Poland ready to open at her touch could turn her eyes from their own bright vision. Appeals and arguments of priests and magnates alike failed to move her. With immense dignity and a quiet resolution born of her conviction that her alliance with William was heaven-sanctioned, she entrenched herself behind two simple statements: she loved William, and their pact was sacred.

Her counsellors were beside themselves. Was all to be lost because of the will of a stubborn child? Though in their hearts they could not but admire her courage, they relentlessly set in motion every influence that might help to break it. Day by day the pressure increased. The priests, with their thoughts fixed on the great conversion, were William's worst enemies.

But her mother approved her cause—so at least she still believed. Alas, when she most needed confirmation and support, home was far away. The Blessed Virgin would help, but, oh, for an hour with her mother! She knew, too, that her mother was distractedly engrossed with difficulties in her own kingdom, where Elizabeth was playing a losing game.

Not only was the beautiful but ill-fated queen regent entangled in the Polish succession intrigue, but she was at the same moment recklessly trying to break off Mary's engagement to Sigismund. In fact, in appearance, at least, she was manoeuvering to marry Mary to two other princes. Sigismund had by his light manners offended her and Hungary, and, feeling their opposition, had fled to his brother, Wenceslas, the half mad king of Bohemia.

After uprisings in both north and south Dalmatia, Elizabeth now faced others. And thus beset, although she had not changed her mind about William, she was afraid to break with Austria. She felt pressed, driven, and powerless to see her way in Poland. Her heart ached for her child. But Jadwiga was young, she reasoned; once these hard first years were past, she would forget them. At the beginning she had besought her trusted counselor, Nicholas Gara, to get the influential Polish Duke of Oppeln and that staunch supporter of the Anjevins, Jasko of Tenczyn, and others in Poland to pledge themselves to give Jadwiga brotherly protection against all harm. More at this time she could not do.

To add to her present distraction, the Duke of Oppeln, who was of German origin and a supporter of

William, was pressing for the Austrian union. And, worst of all, William's father, Archduke Leopold, his patience exhausted, now appeared in Buda. In a conference with him, the queen mother actually set a date for the marriage of William and Jadwiga, promising that it would be celebrated in August of this year, 1385! But her true attitude remained an open secret throughout Europe. Her child, pathetically listening, heard only vagueness, uncertainty.

It was this fact, more than anything else, that helped, as months passed, to wear down Jadwiga's brave resistance. How much longer could she hold out? Then, just as the magnates seemed to be winning, messengers reported that the elegant Prince William, in gleaming mail and long plumed helmet—a picture of the very flower of young knighthood—accompanied by a magnificent retinue of handsome nobles and poets and musicians and soldiers and many supply and gift-laden wagons, was approaching Krakow gate. Victory! Jadwiga's blood bounded! But in Krakow was consternation.

CHAPTER XIV

The Great Renunciation

What was to be done? There was frantic dashing up and down Wawel Hill and from one hurried conference to another in the city, as the nobles tried to plan their course of action. Clearly, they did not dare shut the gates of the city before the Crown Prince of Austria. Nor did they dare lock their intrepid queen inside Wawel walls. With every hour they could feel the mood of the people clarifying, intensifying. It was surging in sympathy toward the young queen. Dread of the Order, enthusiasm for the recently proposed conversion of Lithuania and the achievement of a greater Poland, were swallowed up in romantic excitement kindled by the thought of the reunion of the youthful lovers.

No, Krakow gates could not be closed. But one thing the powerful could and must prevent. They would allow the Habsburg Prince the freedom of the city below, but not of the hill. For once he was a guest in the royal chateau, supporters of the pact would declare the union accomplished.

Thus they reasoned in this beautiful July of 1385. While the queen and her devoted women, counting the laggard minutes, tried anxiously to follow the meetings, and from windows and balconies above to catch some glimpse of the Austrians. For Jadwiga this was not alone her lover, it was home, Buda, coming at last to end her loneliness.

William had covered the distance between the walls of his own and those of Poland's capital in less than half the time it had taken the Hungarians to escort King Louis' daughter from Buda to Krakow. Indeed, from the moment when, after confirmation of rumors of the Polish-Lithuanian negotiations reached Austria, Archduke Leopold determined to put Queen Elizabeth's promises finally to the test, and to retain his son no longer in Vienna, William's advance had known no delay.

Now the gate of Krakow, so often visioned, opened to him. He proceeded with his brilliant cavalcade along Castle street to Wawel Hill, scarcely observing the city's churches and fine palaces in his eagerness to reach the chateau. But the Wawel gate, to his astonishment, he found barred; Castellan Dobieslaw, as mayor of the Castle, had power to open or close the entrance to the royal hill, and he had closed it. William was filled with chagrin and anger—his father's fears, then, had not been unfounded!

He turned back to the city, where he could count on the hospitality of a friend, Gneawosz of Dalewice. It was he who had brought to Vienna Jadwiga's message telling of her danger. He was warmly received in the comfortable house of this Krakovian, which stood at the corner of one of the streets running into the market place. There, with Gneawosz and others, he arranged for the entertainment of his followers. He knew that he would have constantly to be on his guard. With the military commander and castellan, Dobieslaw, and the controlling magnates against him, anything might happen. There was now no doubt in his mind that they would have shut him from the city had they dared. And his beloved—what would they dare with her? How could she and he circumvent this plot to keep them apart?

Krakow seethed with excitement. Here was living poetry. The people's imagination was aflame. This was drama with the elements of dearest fairy tales: the beautiful princess in the tower above, Prince Charming held below—once again youth beating its iridescent wings against the iron of dynastic power and greed. Instinctively they assumed their roles; extravagant rescue plans charged the air.

Very near Wawel Hill, in fact not more than ten minutes walk from its gate, was the Franciscan monastery, with its beautiful church and refectory and its sunny flower and fruit gardens. Monasteries were in these days not only refuges in times of disorder, but popular meeting places at all times. Through intermediary friends, the Franciscans now offered hospitality to their queen. Would she not meet the Habsburg prince within their neutral walls? Continuous royal gardens and orchards ran from Wawel Hill to their own gardens. The queen could walk with her ladies along the tree-shaded July paths from her apartments to their refectory. Prince William and his suite would reach it from the city side, entering by the cloister's main gateway.

This seemed an admirable plan, and one safe from the opposition's hand. The people expressed their delight in an outpouring of gifts to the brown-robed brothers. News of the proposed meetings went winging across Europe and singers and poets and knights from far and near made ready to journey to Krakow to seek a share in them. For this was a situation in key with chivalry's fondest picturing.

At last all was arranged, and Jadwiga, dressed in green and gold, her burnished hair rippling back from her forehead under a gauzy white veil held by the golden circlet of fleurs de lys, her eyes more vividly blue than they had ever been before, left the chateau about noontime with Elizabeth and Constance and others of her court. They rounded the hilltop and took the downward path. And then came a test of training—would they proceed decorously as became a queen and her suite? Or would Jadwiga and Elizabeth, girls as they still were, break from the others and, following the swift beating of their hearts, run along this uniting path! They tried to catch a glimpse of the other company approaching from the market place. But evidently William had already entered the monastery gate.

At the royal-ecclesiastical frontier they were warmly welcomed by the good abbot, in whose brown eyes was a light which showed that his own youth was not yet dead. Declaring that never before had such honor come to this house of Saint Francis, he conducted them beneath pear and apple trees across the courtyard to the church, where all were first to pray. As Jadwiga walked along the inner delicately arched cloister with its frescoes of Saint Francis receiving the stigmata and of Christ treading grapes in the wine-press, she could feel her pulse's throbbing. Once in the chapel, on her knees, her fingers slipping over her beads, she thought she could calm herself. But she could not—William was here! Longing for home, for all that her girlhood had meant—these had their part in the emotion with which in thought she hurried to meet her comrade.

After prayers she and her ladies were escorted again along the frescoed cloister and out into the flower-filled enclosure. From there they passed through an arched doorway, into the long, vaulted refectory whose three windows, as well as the door, gave upon the garden, and whose walls were covered with paintings of the last supper and other meetings between Christ and his disciples. The friendly brothers had brought in so many branches of trees and flowers that Prince William and his Austrian knights seemed hidden in an indoor garden.

But to Jadwiga, as she advanced, William was swiftly distinguishable! Fifteen—grown from boy to man—how handsome he was in his plumed hat and green coat embroidered with the Habsburg eagle, his red silk hose and purple shoes. His eyes were the deep blue she remembered, and his hair, now caught in a net, was still burnished gold. How mature he seemed; and yet how much the dear gentle playmate she had left behind. Jadwiga did not try to hide her happiness. Nor did William conceal his joy. He had not yet seen his betrothed as queen—how tall in her flowing green robe and sheer veil, how truly queenly she was, how radiantly lovely! He felt that he had never before realized the beauty of the lines of the long oval of her face, of her straight, narrow nose and wide, firm mouth with its delicately bowed upper lip. He had always loved her hair. Thus they looked at each other, thus they reclaimed each other.

Jadwiga was indeed radiant. After the year of anxious separation her whole nature rebounded in happy certitude. Like a bough of one of her great trees that had been pulled down and held darkly to earth, and was now suddenly released to spring upward into the field of light, so her spirit leaped to a luminous plane.

The necessary formal courtesies before the company over, the queen and crown prince threw formalities aside, and while their suites exchanged their own greetings, they poured out their eager questioning and replying in the German of their play days. Then in the midst of the bowery greenery, to the gay music of the orchestra, Jadwiga and her handsome fiancé took their places, and the others theirs, at the long, laden tables following the side walls and at others stretching across the ends of the hall. There was room for more than fifty at each table.

The feasting began, each couple eating from one plate. There was music during the courses and between them special merrymaking. Interested as they were in one another and in the beauty of the monastery setting and the lavishness of the entertainment, the guests could yet scarcely turn their eyes from these happy lovers who were so perfectly suited to each other. It was easy to divine what they were so eagerly talking about; not of this hour, but of others passed at Hainburg, Vienna, Visegrád—of King Louis and Dukes Albert and Leopold, of Queen Elizabeth and Mary, of days spent together with their dogs and horses, or on barges on the Danube. The banquet was but a preliminary to greater festivity. When it was over, all joined in dancing, to the accompaniment, not of the orchestra, but of singing.

With the men and women of the noblesse had come, too, members of the bourgeoisie. Many of the brilliantly clad company had with them their cats and dogs and porcupines; someone had presented the queen with a little dog with a silver collar. All admired the gifts which the Habsburg prince had brought his betrothed. Though accustomed to exquisite workmanship they held their breath before the delicacy of the patterned eagles' wings and the jewelled loveliness of the girdle and chain and combs from Vienna. Now they exclaimed over the beauty of other gifts which he distributed among old and new friends.

Between each group of dances, flutes and trumpets sounded again, while more French and Italian wines and gilded sweets were served. And then in the early evening the happy lovers separated, Jadwiga, with her ladies to return to the chateau, William, with his companions, to their lodgings—both to dream of the next meeting.

Through the richly colored weeks of autumn such happy hours were repeated in the good brothers' monastery, Krakow, indeed most of Europe, could talk of little else. As meeting followed meeting, the old affectionate friendship between Jadwiga and William flowered into a veritable passion.

It is not difficult to imagine the state of mind of the council determined to accomplish the Polish-Lithuanian union! Daily, matters grew worse. The strong Duke of Oppeln openly abetted the lovers. And none other than Duke Ziemowit of Mazovia, whose own kidnapping scheme had failed, was known to be sympathetic. Not, it is true, because of any particular sympathy for William, but because he had no reason to love his pagan neighbor, Jagiello, and his savage Lithuanian warriors. It was rumored that some of their supporters were urging the beautiful young queen and her knightly lover to hasten a clandestine, though official, marriage. A closer watch was kept over the chateau entrance.

In December, Ziemowit came with all his court from Mazovia to Krakow, and there signed a formal agreement of peace between his difficult province and the nation. His powerful presence fired the hope of Jadwiga and William. But just one month later, on the 12th of January '86, a Polish mission stood before Jagiello to inform him that all Poland had agreed to accept him as king!

And now came that culminating scene, about which chroniclers differ. Some assert that William, despite surveillance, managed to enter the Wawel, and that Jadwiga, by means of a rope ladder, helped him to reach her apartment—that he was actually fifteen days within the palace before discovery and humiliating escape. Others tell us that just as victory seemed secured, he indiscreetly tried to force an entry to the chateau and that this gave the council their opportunity. At once they placed guards at every door of the chateau. Jadwiga was virtually a prisoner, and tormented by fears for her lover's safety. She remembered the dreadful night of assassination during her grandmother's reign.

A tide too strong for control was carrying her to a great decision. With the news that Jagiello had started with a strong following from Vilno for Krakow, both she and William realized that unless they acted quickly all was lost. Her crown, the ambitions of Church and state—nothing counted now. She would escape from Wawel Hill, marry her lover in the city and flee with him to Austria. Once outside the palace there would be friends to help—but how was she to reach William?

She must rely on a narrow stairway leading to a little door usually open. She hastily made her preparations, Anna fearfully, prayerfully, helping her, and at a certain hour she slipped breathlessly along it. But at the bottom, to her dismay, she found the door barred and guards posted. "Open," she commanded. "We are forbidden." "By whom?" "The Seigneurs." "But I am your queen!" Throwing back her long mantle, she demanded an axe, which they could not refuse, and while they stood stupefied, the young queen beat on the hinges of the door. Blow after blow, she was winning! Then suddenly her hand was stayed. Dimitri of Goray, aged treasurer of her father and uncle, fell on his knees before her as he implored her to respect the memory of these great ancestors.

At first she heard nothing. A terrible struggle was going on within her. With what eloquence must this venerable servant have pleaded, eloquence which in the end caught her ear. With what power did he picture the greater empire and its happy millions rising to call her blessed, as he turned her eyes from her own heart to the heart of Poland. With what zeal did he show the favor of heaven descending on the queen who had brought a whole people into the Christian fold. Was not this conversion more important in heaven than any betrothal pact, however attested? Now he was tearing her heart from her glowing body —did heaven indeed ask this of her? Must she decide alone? Without William? Without her mother? It was not only her love that she was sacrificing, but once again, family, home, girlhood's hopes and certainties —for William was part of these. A wall seemed rising before her to shut her off forever from all she so passionately clung to.

In the end the tears of the old man and those of the beautiful, ardent girl mingled, and he led her, trembling and broken-hearted, back along the narrow stairway to her chamber. She would write William at once begging him to leave the city. She would never see him again.

The next morning she went desolately along the passageway to the Cathedral where she remained all day before the pitying Christ of a great wooden crucifix (marked today "Here knelt Jadwiga") sealing there her supreme renunciation. How utterly love had possessed her the future was to prove. The measure of that young passion was to be the measure of her gift to Poland. Hour after hour she knelt before the cross at whose base lay the red rose of her love. William had her message. He would now be thinking bitterly of her—he could not see her tears nor hear her anguished prayers for his safety.

Nor were her worst fears unfounded. William was indeed bitter and disillusioned. And, in his agony, he could not separate his beloved from the agents of perfidy and injustice by whom he felt himself betrayed. Rightly alarmed, he fled precipitately, disguised as a merchant, confiding his treasure to Gneawosz for safe-keeping.

Through more than five centuries of troubled and tragic history, this scene on the Wawel has remained fixed in Polish memory, celebrated alike in song and legend. Indeed, for Poland the figure of Jadwiga possesses much of the vivid and vital significance that Jeanne d'Arc has for France. Called to splendid and terrible sacrifice these two maids, one a princess and the other a peasant, have become the symbols of the noblest in national hopes and in national faith.

CHAPTER XV

Jagiello Arrives

A door had shut not only on Jadwiga's girlhood, but it had shut, too, on the south. Her star of destiny pointed to the north. Twice as far away as Buda, about five hundred miles northeast of Krakow, in a land of rolling hills and inland waters, lay the Lithuanian capital, the sprawling, low-roofed city of Vilno. It was a city of wood in terror of the torch, which, brandished by pagans of the still precariously held province of Samogitia or by retaliating Tatars or Poles or covetous Germans, had so often turned the low clustering settlement into a holocaust.

Vilno's royal buildings were grouped about a courtyard on the low land between the broad river Vilija which was spanned by bridges built by slaves and serfs, and the sacred wood. They included the wooden chateau whose gardens ran to the river together with accessory houses, a watchtower from which hot tar and boiling water could be poured on a near enemy, and the pagan sanctuary with its perpetual flame. The stables housed thousands of horses. Following the fourteenth century style of castle building, Lithuanian Grand Dukes set a second better protected chateau on one of the three small sandy hills just beyond the lower enclosure. This, because of its irregularities, was known as "Crooked House." From its generously proportioned hall, decorated with knives, animal heads, and handsome furs and embroideries, they looked off across birch, pine and oak forested lands, dotted with lakes, blue in summer and grandly white in winter. A brick fortress topped each of the two neighboring hillocks. These ducal strongholds were surrounded by customary moat and wall, but the series of outrunning ridges gave more protection than walls.

The capital spread far out from the royal enclosure and the sacred wood with its holy oaks and serpents. As in Krakow Castle street connected Wawel Hill with the Market Place, so here in Vilno, Long Road ran from the chateau to the heart of the city. It was bordered by many small wooden shops, and dignified by a few brick buildings.

Long Road led on to a second capital, the important lakeside city of Troki, about twenty miles west of Vilno. Its typical wooden house was rudely constructed, with a huge fire-place built behind a low brick wall in the corner of the living room. A cauldron hung over the fire, and often a cradle hung from another hook in the ceiling. A hole in the low thatched roof served as smoke vent, and a stretched bladder skin as window, if there was one! People slept on the floor on rugs or straw and in the winter housed their animals in a compartment next to their own. There, too, were kept stores of meat and apples, potatoes, beets, and essential hay and grains. Yet no matter how rude the dwelling, it was apt to have an accompanying grace of honeysuckle and hop vine, or was surrounded by lily and rue plots.

The chateau was set on a miniature hill rising beside the lake shore. Its carpets and embroideries rich in oriental colorings and motifs, and gold and silver ornaments, mingled with the spoils of war and chase, witnessed to the wealth of Duke Kiejstut whose particular property this had been. It was now claimed by his handsome son, Prince Witowt, who was destined to become the hero of the new century—already in Witowt's face shone a dream. In their youth, small, lithe Witowt and his more solidly built cousin, Jagiello, had been often together at Troki, where they frequently discussed Witowt's plans for a splendid palace in the new gothic style to be built on the tree-embowered island in the lake. When not at war, they had hunted wolves and boar and buffalo, almost literally living in their saddles.

But this close cousinly relationship was violently broken by the fatal struggle between the powerful Jagiello and his uncle over the inheritance of Olgierd's rights and possessions, Kiejstut lost, for Jagiello, after having called him to a conference, had had him strangled. How successfully the Knights of the Cross had fanned the flame of this fire, no one quite knew; but many were certain that they had a hand in every evil intrigue.

To strengthen their hold on the far-away Dnieper

river plains, other granddukes beside Jagiello's father, Olgierd, had married Ruthenian princesses, who brought with them the civilization of the East and made Ruthenian the court language. Jagiello's mother, Julianna, adored her seventh dark-haired, dark-eyed, "Lucky" son, some said to the extent of spoiling him. At any rate, she had given him a sound body—he was of medium height and strongly set up—and she pushed in every way she could the development of his inherited capacities.

But Lithuanian-Ruthenian culture was not western culture, and the Lithuanian people as a whole were still pagan, shackled by the evils of slavery and polygamy. Therefore, Europe had prayed for the success of the German knights in their crusades. Had the original ambition of these soldiers to win the heathen to Christ, not succumbed to the ambition to add Lithuanian territories to that Prussia for which they were laying the foundation, they might have succeeded in converting this last pagan people in Europe. Lithuania was ripe for conversion. Franciscan missionaries from Krakow, who braved death and met it, had probably done more than any others in preparing the soil for its Christian harvest. Wooden crosses on a hill beyond Jagiello's chateau at Vilno testified to their martyrdom.

During the thirteenth century every ruler of Europe had aspired, as King Louis and Duke Albert had, to share with the White Capes at least one crusade against the northern infidel. But now toward the close of the century, their curious theocracy was so absorbed in secular pursuits that it was the object of fierce denunciation even within the Church itself. Saint Bridget of Sweden was not the only holy person to attack them with tongue and pen of flame. Yet everyone admitted that the Order had been a civilizing influence. Its members had reclaimed the swamps and wastes of the Prussian coastal lands, developed agriculture and trade, and founded cities.

Companies of knights numbering thousands still came from all Christian lands to visit Marienburg, if only to see the red brick walls and spires, and halls rich in stained glass and sculpture and patterned marble floors, lifting above the river, and to enjoy the wine cellars and warehouses and gardens which supplemented the stores that the heavily freighted wagons brought daily to its gates. Without these gates was a supporting city, and within them were military training quarters, agricultural and other schools, and a great variety of workshops and mills. The White Capes were famous for their archery; and their falcons, which they presented as tokens of regard, were coveted throughout Europe. From this center of science and learning they went forth on their mission, now primarily one of conquest of Lithuanian territory.

What a live coal to the imagination were the fantastically far-flung, mobile boundaries of Lithuania! Ethnically small, the country had grown until it reached farther and more vague steppes, over which moved immense human tides. In the lowest Lithuanian, this picture called only to brute warrior covetousness. In the highest—in Prince Witowt, for instance—it awoke a dream—of aggrandizement, yes—but also a dream of himself as a bringer of civilization, of salvation, to heathen peoples. His histrionic eye saw himself in the dazzling role of beneficent arbiter of these yet unstabilized, ferocious eastern hordes.

His cousin, Jagiello, did not thus dream. He was jealous of his father's gains and eager to increase them, and in the division of power among his brothers, tenacious of his own position of leadership. But something deeper was stirring in him; often he was looking westward rather than eastward. Little did that West suspect him of statesmanlike thoughts! The Germans had effectively pointed him out before Europe's eyes as the hairy wolf, the bloodthirsty Saracen of the north. So Europe and Jadwiga believed him to be.

Directly north of Jagiello's capital, at Riga, was another Order, much less powerful than that of the Teutonic Knights. It was the leader of this Order who was one of the first to urge Jagiello to consider the enormous advantages of union with Poland. And why, he asked, with the young Hungarian queen now crowned at Krakow, might not the Grand Duke through this union win this most beautiful woman in the earth's circle as bride?

And simultaneously the Poles were asking the

same question. One of the inevitable, inexorable great moments of history had arrived, and was demanding of a young girl that she become its servant.

So the negotiations had been opened, the treaty of Krewo was signed and assurances were given. Then Jagiello hurriedly prepared to make the great journey. And soon with most of his brothers,—among them Skirgiello, Boris and Korygiello, Swidrigiello and Wigunt, and his cousin, Prince Witowt, and a great company of other princes and boyars, and many long four-wheeled wagons carrying treasure, he passed between the flanking shaggy-haired multitudes shouting their goodbyes, out of the capital, Vilno, and on toward Troki. He travelled south to Lublin where he halted cautiously several days, during which his long friendship with the castellan, Kmita, was founded. From there he proceeded slowly and grandly to Sandomir, each day joined by more Polish nobles. None were more eager to go to meet Jagiello than the members of Poland's army, which included not only the great nobles, but all land owners, the clergy alone being allowed to send substitutes. Each wanted to be the first to see this prospective commander in chief, whose fighting qualities were known far beyond Europe. To the Lithuanian and his party the goal seemed now assured; yet they were keeping a watchful eye on Ziemowit.

From the moment she shut her lover out of her life Jadwiga became only the Christian queen. Once, however, the curiosity of the daughter of Eve spoke again. Jagiello was approaching the city. Was he indeed as hideous as the Germans reported him? She sent for Zawisza of Olesnica, a knight known for his veracity, and charged him, on the pretext of complimenting Jagiello, to go to meet him, to accept no gifts, and to return quickly to report his impressions. Zawisza could make a good report. The pagan, though short of stature, was not ill-appearing. His face was longish, his hair black, his rather small, restless eyes, brilliantly dark, his teeth shining white. His skin was wind-browned because of wild warrior adventures on the steppes, and also because of his passion for the hunt. His voice was low and his speech rapid. Far from being the hairy savage Christians had pictured, he had on the whole a gentle expression, and on this occasion at least, princely manners. It appears that Jagiello, suspecting the knight's mission, had received him with much courtesy, and, probably not without amusement, invited him to accompany him to the bath!

Zawisza's report greatly reassured the queen. But the red words, pagan wolf, scourge, murderer, that had been burned in on her girl's brain, could not be quickly erased. Priests and princes had been striving to erase them, but with little success. If she looked to Hungary for rescue she saw, with anxiety, such dark clouds of threatening catastrophe closing over her mother and Mary, that she knew she could expect little help from them. Often in these moments she seemed to be standing again with William beside the

Danube as together they watched its dark current, rushing, rushing, onward. With what terrible clarity words of dear Scribe John as he interpreted Saint Margaret's renunciation—words at the time rather vague—now sounded in her ears. But had not Saint Margaret after all, had the favored part? Would it not be easier to flee to the shelter and quiet of a convent, back to the nuns of Saint Clara or Saint Margaret, than to remain crowned and sceptered where she was? To face, what? As she asked such desperate questions, she met her father's answering, reassuring look. Had he but lived, how different things would have been! But he *was* looking down upon her! She would have to work things out. In her generous self-forgetfulness, she longed to help her unfortunate mother and sister.

Then the struggle began all over again. No one had yet convinced her that this man coming to take William's place had not at least instigated the murder of his uncle, Kiejstut. Nor could she forget that her father and William's uncle, Duke Albert, counted among their holiest achievements their crusades against this outcast ruler of an infidel people. Jagiello might be outwardly changed but how could he be within? She fled again to her chapel and the Blessed Virgin, and to courage-renewing thoughts of the intrepid saints, Bridget and Catherine.

The greater part of the Diet had gone to meet the grand duke, who approached for the first time not to destroy, but to build. They forgot desolate Jadwiga, forgot everything except that the fact that the dreaded Jagiello was coming to them in peace. They watched his shining cavalcade as if it were somehow miraculously tracing a line of demarcation, shutting off forever the past years of fire and sword. Of all Jagiello's retinue, his gifted cousin, Prince Witowt, most excited their curiosity. Witowt was vivid, active, abstemious in food and drink, though indulgent of other appetites—altogether a fascinating personality. The presence of this son of the murdered Kiejstut, witnessed strongly in the suitor's favor.

On Monday, February 12, 1386, as Jagiello entered Krakow, an excited populace hailed him as their deliverer from the nightmare of ever-threatening invasion. But he heard little, saw little, in his eagerness to be brought at last face to face with the woman who was the light of this new day beginning for himself and his people. He proceeded, escorted by a group of Polish seigneurs, to Wawel Hill.

There was excitement and hurrying to and fro in Jadwiga's apartment as dames and maidens of honor made ready for the reception of the bridegroom. Had this day but come a month earlier, and the preparations been for the handsome young Prince William, they would have been singing and dancing since dawn. Their poor queen—a man twice her age—and not of her world—a rough pagan! But they must not give way to these thoughts. He *was* coming, and he *was* the bridegroom.

Jadwiga herself superintended all details, grateful

for activity. The night had brought her little sleep, but she was determined to fail in nothing. The door that had been barred against the man she had chosen, was now swung wide to the man others had chosen; music filled the courtyard as he approached. She had given her word, when the Lithuanian Grand Duke entered he would find her calm. And so he found her. She bravely took her place on the throne at one side of which stood Duke Wladislaus of Oppeln and at the other Duke Ziemowit of Mazovia. The assembled Polish nobles anxiously searching her face, read on the fine forehead and in the sad eyes only dignity and control—they knew that they could depend on her. Then all eyes turned to Jagiello, advancing now toward the throne. He was clad in a long, straight robe of green velvet, with gold buttons and embroidered down the front with gold, and held by a magnificently wrought red and gold belt which matched his scabbard. His red velvet cape, too, was gold embroidered and furred with ermine. His advance was conventionally timed, yet one suspected in him a certain swiftness and nervousness of temperament. On his long, smooth-shaven face and in his dark small eyes shone an intensity of emotion. Looking up, he saw beauty more wonderful than his dream of it. He dropped to his knees before the girl queen. And she, looking at him, knew that she need not fear this man.

Fortunately, she had little time to think much beyond that. The day following the presentation, Jagiello sent his brothers Skirgiello and Boris to the chateau with magnificent gifts for her of gold and silver and oriental tissues. At court, in the church, in the council, there was a tumult of activity. The speed of the program then launched makes even vaunted present-day pace seem laggard. Only three days after his arrival, the Lithuanian fulfilled the first of his promises. With ceremonies whose import shook the Christian world, the ruler of the fire-worshippers was baptized in Krakow Cathedral by Archbishop Bodzanta of Gnezno, along with his relatives and a large number of boyars, the Duke of Oppeln standing as his godfather. He took the title of Wladislaus II, while his brother, Korygiello, became Casimir; Swidrigiello, Boleslas; Wigunt, Alexander; and others received similarly historic names. Other relatives and followers already baptized in the Greek Orthodox Church held to that faith and kept their old names.

What emotion in Christian Krakow! The influences that would flow from this baptism were incalculable. By it, the Order became an anachronism; yet there in the north its towers rose—what was to be their future? A territory stretching from the Baltic toward the Black Sea and eastward almost to Moscow would now turn its face to the west, toward Rome and occidental culture. Some were already calling Jagiello a second Constantine. With grim humor he had invited Zollner, Master of the thwarted Order, to act as his godfather, but difficulties of travel prevented Zollner from accepting!

CHAPTER XVI

The Wedding Ring of Jadwiga

Jagiello and his suite took over the wagon-roofed chamber and smaller rooms across the court from Jadwiga's apartments, on the level a few steps above and to the rear of the spacious first floor hall opening on the courtyard. A graceful corridor connected this part of the chateau with the large reception rooms, and in addition, there was a secret way. The newcomer had, however, little time to think of his quarters or of the business of getting settled in them, for the drama of the Polish-Lithuanian Union was moving fast. A continuous procession of officials came and went, as they prepared him for succeeding experiences.

There was a like coming and going in Queen Jadwiga's rooms. During the baptismal ceremony, a sense of tremendous forces directing her life—of forces beyond man's understanding or control, had taken possession of her, and was carrying her to the next step which it had seemed utterly impossible she should ever take. She responded as much as she could to the enthusiasm of Anna and Elizabeth and Constance and Katherine and the others over her glorious white bridal robe and veil and royal mantle and indulged them while they lingered lovingly over details of the preparation. How, in their deep hearts, they pitied, adored her; but they, too, were dominated by a realization of the overwhelming significance of all that was passing. Besides, the natural excitement kindled by a wedding could not be quenched.

Sensation upon sensation! On Sunday, February eighteenth, the Church having declared itself free of all responsibility to William (Jagiello was to pay Austria the 200,000 florins promised William's father by King Louis as Jadwiga's dot) the new Christian king of the last pagan country in Europe and the most beautiful woman in the earth's circle were to go together to the altar in Wawel Cathedral. Snow had fallen during the night; courtyard and roofs were a bridal white and the naked trees lifted a glittering tracery of crystal against a blue sky. Krakow jingled with the bells of incoming sleds. The excited, fur-clad throngs were bright-eyed and rosy-cheeked. Knights were as numerous as poppy seed; monks were everywhere, choristers with guitars at their girdles threaded their way through the packed streets. No marriage so important as this had ever been celebrated on Wawel Hill. It seemed that the kings lying in the crypt, those who had lived and died to build the greater Poland, must be conscious of what was transpiring above their silent tombs. All who could possibly gain admittance were inside Wawel walls and the multitude below them timed, minute by minute, the progress of the imagined ceremony.

The flower of the knighthood of Poland and of Lithuania were gathered in the bannered nave; archbishops of Poland, representatives of Rome, officiated at the gleaming altar. Jadwiga's heart might be broken but as she walked down the familiar aisle—the folds of her veil and white robe and crimson mantle spreading far behind her, her queenly head was high. The daughter of Piasts and Anjevins was playing her role. As she knelt with Jagiello before the crucifix, the people dimly understanding, looked on her with awe and reverence. Fate had assigned Jagiello a spectacular role, but through the fifty years crowded with action which remained to him, he clung to the ring she gave him on this day. Henceforth, in song and story, too, it became a symbol, and the union of Poland and Lithuania was called the wedding ring of Jadwiga.

The jubilant company left the Cathedral to recross the snow-covered courtyard and gather in the reception rooms until music called them to the feast. On this commemorative occasion the royal husband and wife entertained together. With Jadwiga's ring on his finger, Jagiello presided with her over the wedding banquet. It was a scene of indescribable splendor. Tables, enjoyed by over a thousand guests, were covered with several white cloths, one of which was removed each time the gilded plates were, and were ornamented with enamelled cups and bowls of silver and crystal, flower-filled. Little gilded trees blossomed, too, along the middle, skillfully concealing in their foliage charms against poison—sealed earth, an eagle stone, a snake's tongue. These would protect partakers from the evil that might lie at the bottom of a beaker. Hundreds of brilliantly clad courtiers served, passing basins and pitchers and towels, as each washed. Trumpets announced courses of meats and fowl and fish, ravioli, fruits, and golden cakes, fine wines and hydromel. Singers and farceurs appeared in the intervals; knights boxed and did athletic turns; jongleurs even entered the hall on horseback—if the tumult grew too great, Jagiello clapped his hands.

The feasting and celebrating continued during several days. There were races and tourneys in the jousting place, dances of knights on horseback, every form of amusement dear to the people. And during all this time Polish and Lithuanian princes were fraternizing. Those who had assisted in arranging the marriage were rewarded with gifts of gold and silver and horses, and of lands as well, of all of which the Mazovian dukes got the lion's share. Of Jagiello's generosity the poet Suchenwirt sang.

"With gold and silver, gorgeous clothes,
And horses with many a roach,
Rewarded were the noble knights
Who him to Krakow brought."

As after the Baptism at Krakow many Lithuanian nobles imitated their Grand Duke's example, so now a whole series of inter-marriages followed his own.

The most important were those uniting the remaining Piasts with the Lithuanian ruling line; Prince Witowt's sister, Anna, was given to John, of the feudal Dukedom of Mazovia, where up to now the name of Lithuania had spelled terror; and Jagiello's sister Alexandra, a great favorite with him, became the wife of John's brother, that Duke Ziemowit who had once planned to kidnap Jadwiga!

March 4th was the coronation day. A new crown, bright with jewels, had been made for Jagiello. Polish nobles, among them Knight Zawisza who two weeks before had gone to meet him, prepared him for this further ceremony. With a ritual whose splendor again taxes the imagination the "barbarian" was received into Poland. These succeeding scenes were three parts of one whole, typifying with cumulative power the significance of the union. How the artist would have painted the triptych!—its central panel representing the coronation, and those at either side the baptism and the marriage, each scene challenging the other with its beauty and meaning.

Because of these events, one of those invisible frontier lines so strangely potent in human history, was suppressed. The consequences of this moment were immeasurable. The boundary of western Europe was pushed far eastward. Polish influence would follow it, Polish desire for expansion, for agrarian development, would be made possible. Also, a barrier was rising to shut off danger from the west. Even today, after five hundred years, this barrier raised against the first wave of the German *Drang nach Osten,* against the Teutonic Knights, precursors of the grenadiers of Frederick and the gray-clad soldiers of Hindenburg, still stands. Abolished temporarily by the partitions, it was restored by the insistence of an American President in the Treaty of Versailles. Peace, and the equilibrium of the world were hidden under the folds of Jagiello's purple mantle. The dynasty of the Piasts was ended; that of the great Jagiellonians begun, and with it that heroic age of Poland which was to last two hundred years.

After the coronation, King Jagiello went down into the city as Jadwiga had done over a year and a half earlier, and before the Hotel de Ville in the Market Place, received the homage of the burghers. After which he delighted them with a series of banquets and tournaments covering several days, quickly proving to them, too, that his would be no niggard rule.

At the time Archbishop Bodzanta was crowning Jagiello, William rode through the gate of Vienna. And even if the dramatic scenes which symbolized the potentialities of her sacrifice were of great solace to Jadwiga, her eyes looked beyond them to the lonely, embittered knight re-entering the city where they had been such happy children together.

And they were fixed, too, with piteous questioning on Buda. These tremendous events were bearing her forward, and neither mother nor sister was near! They seemed still more distant because of terrible news from Hungary, where treason threatened to engulf all that remained of her family. In the preceding year things had come to a head through a plot fomented by the Horváthy family, which had offered the throne to King Charles III of Naples,—that Charles who had succeeded the murdered Queen Joanna and whom King Louis had so carefully pledged to loyalty to his wife and daughters. Elizabeth, hoping to forestall a catastrophe, had herself sent a message to Charles inviting him to visit Hungary. His wife, Margareta, filled with foreboding, urged him not to set out, but the lure of the crown was great and he embarked.

Elizabeth now desperately needed help, so she at last carried through the marriage of Mary and Sigismund. As Charles approached, Sigismund retreated to Bohemia, so that only the two queens went in the gilt coach with their escort to meet him beyond Buda. They invited him to live in the castle, but this Charles declined to do, choosing for the time being a city house as domicile. It was not long before cries of, "Out with women! Heaven sent Charles to be our King!" rang down the streets. And not much longer before Charles was strong enough to force the two women to go to Zékes Fehérvár to witness his coronation. Only three years earlier Queen Mary had been crowned in this Cathedral with her father's crown.

Mother and daughter simply clad appeared shortly before the celebration, and entering the chapel where King Louis was buried and where former scenes were so vividly revived, they sank with tears and sobs on his tomb. The nobles, watching them, could not but be moved. Had Elizabeth and Mary then cried out to them for protection, Charles might have been murdered, not crowned, before the altar. But they did not cry out; they took their places, and sat with their veils gathered closely about them while Archbishop Dimitri proceeded with the ceremony. Later, as the pageant began its march along the excited streets of the capital, an electric storm swept violently over the city. It split the banner of Saint Stephen and shook the palace on the hill to its foundations.

Elizabeth, now bereft of power and listening to bad counsel, sought help in cunning and crime. While she was reading to Charles some of Sigismund's letters, at a sign from Nicholas Gara one present drew a hidden sword and split the king's head almost to his eyes. Elizabeth fainted. In the deep night Charles was hurried to Visegrád, where before the end of the month, at Gara's instigation, and probably with Elizabeth's consent, he was strangled by Forgach, the royal cup-bearer, and later buried on Saint Andreas abbey. He had reigned thirty-six days!

The day after he had been hurried from Buda the city echoed with the cry, "The King of Naples is killed! The rightful Queen Mary is again on the throne!" And the optimistic in the queen's party, blind to the approaching Nemesis, felt that they had extirpated the treason. Such was the home news that reached Jadwiga while, alone, she made her crucial decisions. The report of Charles' burial came shortly after her marriage. Her mind was filled with tormenting concern for her mother and Mary as she faced her new life. It was, indeed, with relief that she turned to the difficulties she and Jagiello and the council of the crown faced in her own kingdom.

King Jagiello had, from the start, favorably impressed his new subjects. On his very coronation day he had confirmed the ancient privileges of the noblesse and accorded new rights, impressing all by his liberality. He would have liked directly afterwards to go to Lithuania to fulfill his major promise—that to convert his people to Christianity; but travel routes across the northern marshes and forests would be impassable until after spring floods had subsided. Therefore, he and Jadwiga decided first to make the tour of their realm. It was important to consolidate support behind the new joint rule as quickly as possible. And so, almost before the embers of celebrating bonfires were gray, they were deep in preparations for the Grand Journey.

With all this activity there seemed to be little time for them to get acquainted with each other, yet they were doing so. To Jagiello, Queen Jadwiga was the radiant symbol of the new world on whose threshold he stood. It was not strange that he should feel that there was something almost miraculous in his possession of this beautiful being, at once girl and woman

—who with each day was becoming less the girl and more the woman. He caught flashes of a joyous youth beneath her seriousness when he saw her laughing with Elizabeth. And one morning when he brought his northern dogs to show her, he thought for a moment that she had forgotten throne and king alike and would run romping out through the door and across the plain to the hills.

But usually she was the mature and dignified queen. What made her seem older, too, to her husband, was the fact that she had long possessed what he was but beginning to acquire. She had the learning, the accomplishments, of a civilization which he coveted for himself and for his people. She understood the mysteries of that religion through which he was to enter a new spiritual world. The priests, to be sure, were his teachers, but his true teacher was his girl wife, already known across Europe for her piety. Through her alone the golden key to the future had been placed in his hands.

His ways were more brusque, ruder, than her father's, nor had he any of the elegance or charm of William; but his heart was kind. This, Jadwiga early discovered. He was simple and unassuming. Another ruler over such vast territories as Lithuania's, holding them by far-shining courage and skill, might have flaunted his pride, but in Jagiello there was no arrogance. He was ever looking not at the past but toward the future.

It was, in fact, his spirit of self-depreciation, which

gave him that certain wistfulness, which had first caught Jadwiga's sympathy. This man of rough superabundant vitality seemed burdened by a consciousness of the superior advantages of those born into the western environment, and to suffer inwardly from a sense of inferiority. He could not easily read or write as others about him could, and because of this and other deficiencies, often imagined criticism or slight when none was intended.

These things the young queen had not expected to find in the warring Lithuanian. They called to her generosity. She would not merely outwardly, but truly, share everything she had with him—his strangeness must be exorcised. And Jagiello himself was as generous in his personal relationships as he had proven in dispensing gifts and privileges after the recent celebrations. He was as quick to acknowledge fine qualities in others as he was to confess a fault of his own. His modesty at times amounted to humility; he was ready to fall on his knees to ask pardon for a lack or error on his part. One thing she had noticed—that whatever longing or questioning saddened him, it disappeared as soon as he was in the saddle. Once on his horse, his eyes kindled and confidence shone from his face.

Warning voices, to be sure, were not lacking; voices counselling Jadwiga against inviting future disillusionment by placing too much faith in first reactions to a great experience. Even though Jagiello's forehead was broad and high, they said, and his countenance stamped with nobility, the small, dark eyes were too mobile, suggesting that underneath them was hidden an irritable soul. But as yet Jadwiga had no evidence of this.

CHAPTER XVII

First Tour of the Land

In their private life, then, the young queen and the older king found their preferences congenial. Jagiello was as simple in his tastes as Jadwiga, as unostentatious, as eager to practise the self-denial and fasting prescribed by the Church. However, since in public, a brilliant effect counts, and since his imagination envisaged a dramatic expression of the magnitude of the royal function, the Lithuanian liked to travel accompanied by thousands of knights. Nor could his or their apparel or the trappings of their horses be too richly ornamented. And particularly on this first tour of the realm the progress must be attended by all possible splendor. Not only the king makers of Little Poland and the immediate royal retinue, but troops from Krakow and Sandomir would accompany him.

The entire court machinery and the co-operative activity of Krakow's guilds and merchants were set in motion to secure for the long cavalcade an appearance that would fill the eye. Armorers, tailors, shoemakers, saddlemakers, sword-makers, silver and goldsmiths, jewellers—who had not a feverish part in the outfitting? Apothecaries and caterers of all sorts of supplies assisted. And a flock of useful workmen pressed for places in the train.

Jadwiga, despite the tragic weeks culminating in her supreme renunciation, and despite her daily distressed concern for her mother and Mary, was strong and eager for work. As for Jagiello, he lived on action, and although in those days a man past thirty was accounted already old, he felt young. They arranged the affairs of their separate courts and personally attended to innumerable details of the preparations for the formidable journey. To his jewelled coat of mail and silver helmet the new king added his favorite sword, whose hilt was set with turquoises and rubies. And Jadwiga got ready the little travel altar and the carved ivory box holding her smaller necessities, which she had brought from Buda. They faced four months of continuous visiting and celebrating, and of successive audiences and conferences; for they could scarcely hope to return home before August. They would stop in the royal chateaus, or in abbeys or castles of the nobles, all of whom were obliged to give hospitality to the ruler and his suite, who, however, furnished or paid for the food.

When all was ready and the historic procession wound its way down Wawel hillside, the magnificent appearance of the royal pair, the gleaming mail and plumed helmets of the knights, the sweeping caparisons of the horses, and the multicolored costumes of the accompanying groups made an imperial picture. Bells sounded and the capital rang with cheers as they passed along Castle street and made the tour of the Market Place. After the events of the past few weeks people had felt that all emotion was exhausted, but it welled afresh as the added picture expressed the reality of the union. What development might Krakow not expect under the protection of the combined power symbolized in this pageant? Then the glitter and the glory passed out through the city gate, and the Jagiellonian review of the realm had begun.

Small wonder that excited throngs all along the way pressed to see this procession. Here was the most beautiful, the most holy, and also the saddest queen in the world; the little queen who had given them her heart. And beside her rode the wolf, the infidel—now tamed and become Christian because of her. The people recognize and love poetry. Here was living poetry.

This was one aspect of the moving picture. Another was the practical one, made up of succeeding scenes in which the royal pair received oaths of allegiance, confirmed privileges or gave rewards. The journey across Small Poland was a continuous jubilant success. But in Great Poland, where searing memories of Lithuanian invasions had not yet had time to cool, and where resentment over the failure of Ziemowit's candidacy still smouldered, the way was not so smooth. It was only considerably later that the nobles of Great Poland received the concessions now granted to those of Small Poland. Concessions too generous, for they meant increased independence to the aristocracy, independence which represented a steady pulling away from centralized authority. Such grants testified to the progress of that movement to curtail the power of the crown which was to prove so disastrous to this Slavic country. King Louis had yielded earlier to similar demands in order to gain consent to the Anjevin succession. Among other things, Jadwiga's father had agreed, in the pact of Kassa in 1374, to exempt the nobles from all taxation except two Polish groschen per hide of land and to compensate them for all military service given beyond Polish borders. Now Jagiello further limited the monarchial power by freeing the nobles of Small Poland from their ancient responsibilities toward royal fortresses and royal castles.

But more revealing than an account of grants and vows is a love story that has run down the centuries, which grew out of the visit of the king and queen to Gnezno, the venerated cradle of the Polish Kingdom. When they arrived, following customary ruthless practise, their retinue fell on the country, seizing the cattle and goods of the peasants for their needs. The unhappy peasants came weeping to complain of this spoliation, and demanded restitution. Struck by the profound emotion of Jadwiga, Jagiello went himself to investigate, and did prompt justice. "Be consoled," he said to her on returning. "I have given back to these poor people their possessions." "Yes," replied the queen, "but who will give them back their tears?" She knew the meaning of tears.

At Eastertide, they had reached northwestern Poznan, which on this occasion outdid itself in the solemnity of its preresurrection services and the beauty and joyousness of those of the resurrection Sabbath. This was Jagiello's first participation in the elaborate Catholic Easter rites. Though he found it difficult clearly to understand their varied meaning, their mysticism stirred his imagination. For he had imagination and a sensitiveness quickly responsive to beauty. This had made him, always, alive to the loveliness of the out-of-doors, to the singing of birds and to the silences of his dark northern forests.

During these days Jadwiga described to him Easter celebrations at Visegrád with their accompaniment of elaborate gift-giving; for Easter, more than Christmas, was the gift-giving festival. As a girl she had prized most the yearly white lamb the shepherds had brought her. Jagiello was intensely interested in what she told him of her country, not only because of herself, but because Hungary now was his most important ally. And for similar reasons she listened eagerly to the continuous unfolding of the story of Lithuania.

Glimpsed pictures of that idolatrous worship the cross was soon to sweep from the land both fascinated and repelled her. At this time of the year priests foretold what the harvest would be by making sacrifices on altars of the fire god, Perkinos, altars which stood under the largest oak trees of the forest, and were tended by white-robed virgins. The most solemn part of the springtide ceremony was conducted by the high priest, rarely seen, who sacrificed a pure white horse in the presence of the people. For this rite he himself wore white raiment and a three-cornered hat on top of which shone a golden ball.

However disrupted Lithuania might appear to be, there was union through this white-haired high priest of the eternal fire, and the formidable hierarchy under him. He dwelt in the deep forest near the highest sanctuary of Perkinos, from whose oak-enclosed square he sent out his commands inscribed in a kind of runic lettering on crooked staves which the priests carried. The fire altars were insatiable, at times demanding even human sacrifices; insatiable, too, were the coiled serpents.

From Perkinos, the order of gods descended—gods of moon and stars, waters and winds, birth and death, and re-incarnation after death, on down to strange, restless, ever-present or ever-distant spirits called laumes,—a blend of elf and troll, witch and nixy—with whom every child and grown-up lived most intimately. Jagiello's tales of the pranks of these laumes, who were as changeable as the weather, were inexhaustible.

He himself had already discarded pagan charms for Christian relics, but that there was still confusion in his mind was proven by an incident of this journey which caused no little amusement. In Plock Cathedral, in Mazovia, where a religious spectacle was in progress, the king asked what a certain image represented, and on being told, "The Christ," he replied, "I will light a candle for him." Shortly after this he inquired about another representation. That, he was told, was the devil. Equally responsive, he again said, "I will light a candle for him." Whereupon a priest, crossing himself, quickly cast the unholy candle forth from the Cathedral and tried to make clear to the royal mind his reason for doing so!

Just before leaving Krakow, Jagiello, with Jadwiga's consent, had sent his trusted brother, Skirgiello, from Poland back to Lithuania, where his half-brother André was darkly conniving with the Order. The situation in his homeland, which was perennially disquieting, had become alarming. Angry Duke Leopold had not been idle in Vienna. And when Prince William had addressed a letter to all Christian rulers of Europe asking them to join with him and Austria in an effort to punish Jagiello for the rape of his promised bride, the Teutonic Knights had been quick to reply sympathetically. They and Austria, along with certain German and Russian princes, had made a punitive alliance. And both the Order, and certain Russian princes who feared the Grand Duke's increased power, had crossed Lithuanian borders. Anxiety because of this, and other news, made the king and queen decide to return as soon as possible to the capital.

When they reached it, in August, they found the danger dramatically averted. An event unforeseen by them, an event beyond their borders, had broken the back of the alliance. That event was a further success of the Swiss in their struggle for independence. On the field of Sempach in July, 1386, the mountaineers had overwhelmed Duke Leopold, who had attacked them. William's father was killed, and though the Swiss lost but few, two thousand soldiers and seven hundred of the first knights of Austria lay dead on the battlefield. This disaster caused Zollner, Grand Master of the Order, to decide that the weather was too bad for advance into Lithuania! Only the Teutonic Knights of Livonia and the Russian princes of Smolensk crossed the frontier, leaving desolation in their path. And these, Jagiello's brother, Wigund, who had hurried north from Krakow, defeated in a bloody battle.

Relief at this escape from immediate danger of invasion was, however, all but forgotten in the dismay caused by appalling reports from Hungary. There, Elizabeth, worn out physically and mentally and powerless to avert approaching tragedy, had decided to go with Mary to Croatia, where Nicholas Gara thought the presence of the two queens would quell the rebellion that had been seething ever since the murder of Charles. After that they were to make a recuperative visit to Gara's castle in Dalmatia.

Elizabeth started with him and Mary and but a few attendants, in the famous gilt coach for the south. At Diakovar they were suddenly surrounded by Croats, and deserted by most of their attendants. Nicholas, however, to the end the loyal defender of

King Louis' family, leaped on to one of the carriage steps to protect the queen with his body. But by a swift sword he was decapitated and his head thrown into Elizabeth's lap. With lifted hands, she implored John Horváthy, leader of the plot, to spare Mary, and let herself, alone, suffer for the crime. But Horváthy remained unmoved. He intended to turn both women over to Margareta, Charles's widow, and to establish her son on the Hungarian throne. So he took his royal captives to Krupa prison in the Liccaer mountains, and later on to Novigrad. From there he planned to conduct them to Apulia, where queen Margareta had demanded they be brought to her alive. The Venetians, however, had no intention of permitting the union of Naples and Hungary, and they began bombarding Novigrad from the sea. And as a warning to this attacking fleet, the queen regent was brutally murdered in Mary's presence. Mary was held a prisoner while Sigismund, who throughout had been slow and ineffective, was with his army trying to reach her.

Jadwiga, like a ship driven between gale and gale, tried desperately to steady herself. Her beautiful, her gay, her adored mother gone! What terror and anguish must have filled those last hours! What terror Mary must still hourly be suffering! What an ending of Louis' hopes, what a close to the happy, promising years at Visegrád! She hung her room in black, covered her bed with black; midnight and dawn found her on her knees before the Madonna in her chamber.

She prayed, too, for William, mourning the death of his father. She had heard tales of his bitter complaint of her, and though she suffered from them, in her heart she felt only pity for him. Even now they were only on life's threshold, and yet how darkly distant was the river, how far off Vienna, Visegrád, Buda. An iron curtain had dropped down, shutting off those happy scenes forever.

CHAPTER XVIII

The Great Conversion

Personal sorrow must not affect affairs of state. Besides, Jadwiga's unselfishness would not permit grief of her own to cast its shadow on others. Wawel courtyard continued to be the scene of the arrival and departure of bright companies, and though the queen did not participate in the dancing and gaieties, she encouraged her court to do so. During these days of mourning, Elizabeth was with her more frequently, and Constance and others daily sought ways of expressing their sympathy. She and they were working early and late now on the many altar cloths and vestments to be sent to Lithuania. After busy hours, they frequently walked in the early twilight in the gardens. Their favorite path was that along the side hill, dropping down toward the gate leading to the Franciscan orchards, the tree-shaded path they had traversed so joyously when William was in Krakow.

On certain days the king came to the queen's apartment to breakfast with her, partly to cheer her, partly because he wanted to talk over with her the plans for the great evangelization; but mainly because he found her appealingly beautiful, robed now in severe black with her marvelous hair falling loose over her shoulders. At such times Jadwiga felt his adoration of her, but she could not give again what she had given William. She felt for the king something akin to what she had felt for her father. While, young as she was, she surrounded him with a certain maternal care. It was religion which more than all else united them by its mystic bond. This, on her part, took the place of love.

Just humanly they needed each other. Both were surrounded by their suites, living most of the day in the presence of others, holding conferences, listening to counsellors; but, after all, this was *their* kingdom, and since in it they were both strangers, in reality they had but each other. In these first months she, in her warm and generous youth, was eager to give, he equally eager to take, to learn. However rough or crude his ways, beneath them was a desire not to be different, which meant constant adaptation—he was taking on a protective coloring.

On such intimate mornings king and queen discussed those small matters which are the essentials of co-operative living. They exchanged reports of their kitchens, of cooks and tailors, of the health and behavior of their courts, they chatted about late visitors and last gifts. Jadwiga's training at Buda had prepared her to direct with a live interest the housekeeping of her part of the chateau. She had great pride in the books in which expense items were meticulously recorded.

Moreover, she had a natural feminine pleasure in discovering and satisfying her husband's preferences; and on these days of informal breakfasting she produced his favorite platter of scrambled eggs heaped with sausages, honey and pears and other fruits. Even in these private apartments all things, plates, linen, food, garments, were brought to the king only by trusted aids. He wore defensive Christian relics (and still some pagan amulets!) and held to his belief in his luck; but vigilance had to be thousand-eyed—poison was a familiar weapon, employed with especial success in loosely-held Lithuanian territories. Life, here, was not soft, since danger was never absent.

In all conversations, Lithuania was uppermost. Jagiello had never before been away from his country for so long a time; and knowing existing rivalries, his mind was unquiet. Moreover, with each day the zeal of the evangelist grew. The neophyte who was attending three, sometimes five, masses a day, and taking sacraments, was impatient not only to keep his promise, but also for his new religion's sake, to convert his people.

Jagiello wanted his young wife, who had tried to re-create Hungary before his eyes, to see Lithuania. He pictured to her the country, as it appeared from some high viewpoint, a land of wooded slopes and sky blue lakes, of fertile meadows where great herds grazed, sandy river plains, and amber-sown coastal margins. It was patterned by fields of flax and dotted by brown villages in which women wore clothes partly like the men's and shared their labor. He matched her Danube with his Niemen; the brilliancy of her southern skies with the serenity of his paler northern heavens; the Hungarian forests with Lithuania's incredible, myth-peopled regions of conifers and oaks whose interlocking branches often formed giant roofs shutting out sun and rain. There ranged droves of roaring bison, pride of the Lithuanian world, mighty-antlered elk and gleaming-tusked boar. He had long worn a belt of the skin of a bison he had killed, as a talisman against sword and fire.

These uncharted forests were home to him. He had often with his own axe helped his men cut a cautious way through ever-recurring curtains of convolvulus and ivy, or in sunnier birch and alder thickets had torn an opening through knotted hopvine barriers. The forests had the gentler aspect, too, of wild orchard and garden; for one gathered there apples and pears, berries, mushrooms, and a myriad lilies and herbs, among them the spicy rue that all brides wore. Bees swarmed in hollow tree trunks and there was a wealth of smaller game in the brush and of fish in the waters. Larks and nightingales and the popular grayish-brown cuckoo, and a host of smaller birds so filled the air with song that the Order, when it set its first fortress inside a violated Lithuanian frontier, had called it Vogelsang!

Such accounts were fascinating. There were moments when, as they considered the immensities of nature, both king and queen saw their fate as in some mysterious way part of the whole elemental scheme. Especially in the mind of the king, so long a Pantheist, such suggestion was vivid. What unseen power had moved him down from his rivers and forests, and this beautiful young girl up from her own Hungarian plain to unite them thus at Krakow?

While they waited for the ice bridges to form over the trackless marshes, Queen Jadwiga was increasingly occupied with pious works. She went often down into the city to visit churches and convents and the hospitals she was developing there. Recently she and the king had gone together to review one of the capital's favorite festivals, that of the guild of raftsmen. They watched it from the Hôtel de Ville in the Market Place, delighted with the gaiety of the crowd. All along Castle street they had passed long, narrow, straw-bedded wagons of peasants rattling into the city; had admired the black and white sheepskin coats and caps of the men, and the brilliantly woven shawls and kerchiefs and full skirts of the women, many of whom were on foot. Pride of land and family spoke in these costumes. Flowers of the fields and leaves of the forest mingled with patriotic and religious symbols in their designs of flamboyant beauty.

Now all were crowding as near as possible to the fun-maker, a man who in the quaint disguise of a Tatar, carried the wooden figure of a horse in trappings tied to his waist, and stalked clumsily about among them, imitating a horseman and dealing jocular blows with a mace ending in a cloth knob. Each blow won a laugh or a shout. During the merry-making, many persons came to offer sheaves of flowers and other gifts of field or loom to their queen. The hearts of the people went out to her—in her somber black—they adored her.

After the festival she and Jagiello visited the early gothic Cathedral of Saint Mary, beside the Market Place, stopping outside to watch the gleaming pigeons fluttering between the Cathedral and the lovely little shrine of Saint Barbara nearby. Two men and a woman, being punished by Krakow for "immoralities," were chained by an iron collar set in the Cathedral wall for that purpose, and Jadwiga was moved by their gestures of appeal. This was a customary punishment for offenses against morality or ecclesiastical laws; as was whipping or being exposed in a cage.

In more serious criminal charges, after the jury had heard the witnesses, the prisoner was cast into a dark cell below the town hall, at the farther end of the square, and from there conducted by the executioner and his assistants to the torture chamber, known as the Kabat, where he was thrice tortured to force confession. Then the judge gave the verdict. And the accused had yet to be tried by Ordeal. If found guilty of an offense punishable by death, he was taken outside and beheaded—with a magnificent sword! or hung, or broken on the wheel, burned, or otherwise dispatched.

Tender-hearted as she was, Jadwiga suffered whenever an execution took place. She had already interceded and was often in the future to intercede with the Krakow council for the condemned; for it was the city council which administered this mediæval justice. Inhuman as it was, it had been lifted from much more irregular practice by Casimir the Great's codification of laws and establishment of courts. And both Jadwiga and Jagiello were determined to carry forward these and other reforms in trial and punishment. They particularly wished to increase the dignity and power of the supreme court, which sat in Krakow.

They had frequently to go beyond the capital to honor popular fêtes like this, or to receive allegiance, grant privileges, and perform other official business. From the beginning of their reign they worked tirelessly for the development of a unified Polish state, which must go hand in hand with the larger movement of the Polish-Lithuanian union. And nothing helped more in this effort than their personal presence among their people.

By January the northern winter was so far advanced that ice had built glittering passageways across the miles of lake and marsh that separate Poland and Lithuania. At last Jagiello could make ready to start on his mission of evangelization. Hardly a Christian Pole but would have pressed for a place in the pilgrim line had he thought he could win one. Group by group the fortunate ones assembled. Among them were all the relatives who had lingered in Krakow, the two dukes of Mazovia and many other nobles, Archbishop Bodzanta, Bishop John Radlica, representatives of the higher clergy, and a great company of Franciscan monks whose fraternity had fertilized Lithuania's pagan soil with their blood. Many priests carried little bags holding incense and burners and other ceremonial accessories —what would there not be to do when a whole people was brought to Christ? With all of these the king was ready to set out for his homeland. Prince Witowt and Skirgiello and other Lithuanian nobles had gone ahead to make advance preparations and to receive the royal company.

Krakow had scarcely slept during the days preceding the departure, the very horses seemed to sense the importance of this journey. Queen Jadwiga and her women, having finished last stitches, saw with immense satisfaction their splendid cloths added to the chalices and bowls and crosses, the pictures and other treasure destined for the churches still to be founded. As with crucifix and banner and chant the holy cavalcade got under way, on the Sadomir-Lublin road, the queen, watching and waving, tasted the sweet fruit of sacrifice. In Poland's varied and brilliant history there is no greater moment than this in which it sent the consecrating cross to Lithuania.

What a spectacle at Vilno, on the plain and on the low hills beside the Vilyia River during this famous winter of 1387! On Sunday, February the seventeenth, the procession, led by Jagiello, wound up the icy, slippery path of the hill on whose summit rose the image of the red-eyed fire god, Perkinos, and where on an altar burned the perpetual fire. The crowd, scarcely breathing, waited,—would not a bolt from heaven strike dead these profaners of this place of the gods? But no thunder sounded, no bolt flashed. The zealots fell to work; some monks seized axes and under their blows the wooden image of the fire god was smashed to bits. Others from vases poured streams of water over the fire guarded through generations. And as incense rose in clouds through the crystalline branches, where the false god had stood, a cross was planted. The king and the mitered bishops and the brown-robed Franciscan brothers and as many as could press about them, overcome with emotion, knelt in the snow and a mighty Te Deum rose to the skies.

From the hill they descended to the sacred wood, and again the people watched fearfully, breathlessly —would there not now be a sign? And the gods of the oaks and the serpents issue forth to annihilate all? Priests brought the holy oaks crashing to earth and killed the sacred serpents. And there was no sign. Always the tense crowds tried to keep their eyes on the chief stranger-priest in gold vestments, with a tiara on his head and a crucifix in his hand, leading the others. Then the procession wound toward the river bank and the glorious work proceeded. Here was a ruler personally undertaking to convert his people; for Jagiello assisted in proclaiming the new religion himself first beside the Vilyia and thence outward among the congregated multitudes. He knew the language and the customs of his Lithuanians; everywhere he interpreted for the missionaries. As the thousands surged forward for baptism, priests were lacking to serve them individually, and converts had to be taken to the river bank in groups.

After baptism they were given Christian names, and many, especially among the older people, received from the king white linen mantles, symbols of the new purity. He had brought these from Krakow along with other gifts; for after the long autumn festivities, supplies in the north were low and it was well to carry along corn and other welcome necessities. To facilitate name-giving, one whole group was christened with the name of John, another with Stanislaus or Paul, others became Catherines or Margarets or Dorotheas. Thirty thousand were baptized in this way, as from all the region rose the triumphant chants and prayers of the clergy, to whom the heavens seemed to be opening.

The pagan temple near the royal chateau was destroyed and beside the ruins Jagiello laid the cornerstone of the Catholic Cathedral. Here, early on this holy Sunday, he had the same mass read that was read at his coronation. From Vilno he rode out far over the land, spreading the good work. The bishopric of Vilno was created, with parish churches at Krevo, Keszagole, Miednicki, and other towns—seven in all. Its first bishop was the Franciscan Vasylo, a Pole and a former confessor of Jadwiga's grandmother. Soon afterwards, Rome, which had for so long and until so recently urged crusades against the Saracens of the north, sent a message to their one-time outcast chief. "We are very happy," wrote Pope Urban VI, "that so great a number of pagans have received the holy spirit."

And then men fell to carving wayside crucifixes and shrines, and women to embroidering. How many churches and chapels and cloisters must be built, how many feasts instituted, how many chalices and monstrances and banners be made ready! Here was something tangible and easy to perform. But suddenly to cease consulting the gods of their fathers and to approach this new God—that was a different matter.

Jagiello did not stop with the mere fulfillment of his promise. On similar occasions rulers have used religious reform to augment their own power. He, however, did not take, but gave. Three days after he laid the foundation of the Cathedral, in his chateau beside the Vilyia he signed an edict—a document remarkable in its conciseness and force—which became the charter of Lithuanian liberty. It secured to all his people property rights and equality before the law, and assured them a share in the results of their labor and in the joys of the family. A man could now dispose of his possessions, and a father marry his daughters and relatives as he wished and transmit his property to his widow or his children. Jagiello's subjects were freed in the future from all forced labor for their princes and held responsible for only such works of general utility as the construction of fortresses, and for military service. In addition, judges were to be appointed for all the country, who must, without the intervention of the Grand Duke, receive complaints and pronounce decrees, as under the laws operating in Poland. Thus, in this tremendous hour the Lithuanian became not only a Christian, but a citizen.

And all this was brought about in peace, without the unsheathing of a single sword, simply as a consequence of Jadwiga's sacrifice. This was her victory and her reward.

CHAPTER XIX

GROWING INDEPENDENCE

WHILE Jagiello astonished the world with his swift and sweeping emancipation of his people, Jadwiga thrilled it by launching an intrepid expedition to recover from Hungary—her own country—fertile Red Ruthenia, crossed by great trade routes seeking out Lvov. This land, part of which is better known today as Galicia, had been added to Poland by her great uncle, King Casimir. Back in 1340 he had incorporated Halicz and Lvov, and later, all of Volhynia and other lands. This acquisition had proved a turning-point in Polish aspiration, since its thinly peopled expanses invited colonization eastward. It had been ravaged by the Tatars and its population decimated; but Nature's generosity to its soil assured recovery, and new colonists flocked there to replace the earlier ones. Jews and Armenians dominated its trade. Synagogue and mosque alternated in the cities with Greek orthodox churches and there were Catholic spires; for German burghers, too, had settled there.

When Jadwiga's father, King Louis, was joint ruler of Poland and Hungary, Red Ruthenia had properly formed part of his dominions; but with the crowns again separate, the situation was changed. Should Poland look quietly on while Hungary now sought to appropriate this territory? Inexperienced though she was, Jadwiga felt that she herself must act. Tales of the young queen's wisdom and holiness were being sung across the continent. Now she was to appear in a new rôle, which would early answer the question in the minds of many, as to whether, after her marriage, she would act only through the king.

While Jagiello was still in Vilno, without hesitating, without, it is said, even seeking his advice, Jadwiga decided to go in person with her troops to the disputed territory. It was no easy decision. And though the controlling officers of the administration had determined on this course, Jadwiga had her own independent part in the agreement.

In this action she was taking a stand against her family; for it was Mary's husband, King Sigismund, who was attempting to hold the coveted grain country, claiming it as part of Mary's inheritance from her father. Unhappy Mary was still in prison in Dalmatia, which increased the difficulty of the situation; but while Jadwiga tried to spare her sister's feelings, she was convinced that her first duty was to proceed with all firmness and speed.

The best of the knighthood of Poland, the select of its nobility, made up her winter army, which was accompanied by a crowd of aids and entertainers. It represented the power of this régime; for with it rode such administrative officers as Castellan Dobieslaw and his son; Jasko of Tarnow, Palatin of Sandomir; Spytko of Meltzyn, Palatin of Krakow; Sedziwosz of Schubin, Palatin of Kalicz, and Gneawosz of Dalewicz, William's former friend. The queen, wearing a sable coat and sable hood and gloves, and glowing with youthful charm, conducted the campaign across the snow-covered hill and plain country on horseback, only exceptionally riding in the state carriage. It would be difficult to describe the enthusiasm of the troops, as she rode thus with them; her soldiers adored her. In a short time the leaders of the Hungarian troops garrisoned on the land were fleeing before them.

There were engagements in certain places, but in most towns, because of her conciliatory attitude and her generous concessions, the warrior queen was well received. As she advanced, she accepted vows of allegiance, not as conquering enemy, but as legitimate ruler, returned. The important towns of Przemisl, Jaroslaw, Grodek, and others swore loyalty, and on February twenty-second she entered Lvov, City of the Lion, where amidst moving scenes the many-tongued people swore allegiance. This they were ready enough to do if they were assured security in their privileges and in their pursuit of trade. Armenians, Jews, Tatars, Germans, had not only their separate churches, but in separate quarters preserved their individual customs; they would brook no interference in these matters.

Volhynia, Podolia, and subsequently other provinces, were thus retrieved. Beyond them stretched that Ukraine which was to become the granary of Russia. Much of the soil in smaller, ethnic Poland was poor; here, on marvelous rolling fields, agrarian longings could find satisfaction. Poland already traded in wood and other raw materials with Hungary and Italy. This territory insured commercial relations with the Orient. For the Galician-Volhynian plains were the trade rendezvous of East and West; at their crossroads Nurenberg and Danzig merchants met those from beyond the Urals and Carpathians. The Black Sea would now be an assured economic objective; Polish enterprise could link it with the Baltic and make "Poland from sea to sea" a reality.

Here acted no merely embroidering and housekeeping queen; this imperial gesture proved to all how thoroughly qualified the girl sovereign was to watch over the empire's interests. It throws light on the long debated question as to the precise nature of the joint rule inaugurated with the "wedding ring of Jadwiga"—one of those fascinating open questions in history. Queen in name only, or, in fact, which was she?

The picturesque queen-led army, as soon as its main objectives were secured, turned back toward Krakow to meet Jagiello and enlist his help against still recalcitrant cities. Powerful leaders had accompanied him from Lithuania: Jury of Belz, Vassily of Pinak, Fedor of Wladimir, and many more. And they now journeyed with him from Krakow to complete Jadwiga's work.

One thing alone marred Jadwiga's satisfaction in this victory—it estranged her from Mary. But fortunately it was not long before the two sisters (who had only each other) were reconciled.

The queen gave much thought now to plans for the development of the east Galician territory, the east, which had been so ravaged by the Tatars. There was room for all who had accompanied her and for others who had played prominent parts in the last few years to find reward there, yet she wanted to choose wisely, to place men in control who were alive to the needs of the people. The wife of Casimir had been good to them, had won their love, and they looked on the coming of her great niece as of happy promise. She must not disappoint them. And most important of all, she must send to them priests and teachers. The Benedictines would welcome the chance to begin there the beneficent work which they had done and were still doing in Hungary and in Poland.

Jagiello was often absent from the capital, either on business for Lithuania, which by the terms of the union he continued to rule separately, or for Poland. During one of his absences such a cataclysmic storm broke over beautiful Galicia that some in the palace asked if he could ever return. Winds swept in from the east in fury, whirling what seemed whole plains of dust across the darkened city below, till all was blotted out. As Jadwiga watched from a balcony, the skies seemed to be revolving about her, the earth rolling under them. She had encouraged several of her women to seek refuge in the little chapel across the courtyard, dedicated to the first Christian missionaries to Poland, Felix and Adauctus. Others had fled to the royal burial crypt below the Cathedral. But she herself refused to be drawn inside.

After obliterating dust came rain, rain such as she had never before seen, sheets of it thrown from the heavens to earth and blown back again toward the heavens, while forked lightning netted the scene with fire. It was God's world and He ruled it for His people's good, but the human mind was not able to read the meaning of things. In her short life she had felt the power of invisible forces she could neither understand nor control. Here were wind and water and fire at work in their blinding might. She did not try to explain why, but she was lifted above fear; she felt comfort, exaltation. Even the tormenting question of why God had visited upon her the curse of barrenness was silenced.

Then, suddenly, all was still and bright. There was need of no further concern about the king and his men. She went now herself across the soaked courtyard to the Cathedral, and after her prayers, down to the crypt, where among her dead kings Poland's ideals and hopes were most alive. This experience stirred solemn thoughts. The great house of Anjou in Hungary, the house of her father Louis, and her grandfather Charles Robert—where was it? Mary, though freed from the prison that had held her ten months, and now married to Sigismund, had no children. Poland's future, the continuance of all Jagiello and she were building, depended on her. She fell on her knees beside Casimir's tomb—oh, for a son, a daughter! Would not heaven hear her prayer?

She returned to the chateau to prepare for Jagiello's return. It was the queen's custom, when the king returned from an expedition, to go with members of her court to meet him so that they might enter the capital together. Indeed, the character of their official relations won the praise of all. Jadwiga, like her father, King Louis, had striking personal dignity, which Jagiello greatly respected; he, too, had a high conception of the dignity of his office. "Like the cock which is ready to crow by night as by day, the king must be a king by night as by day," he said. He spoke little, guarding his words, "Which go forth from the mouth as small birds and return as camels."

Yet it was difficult to convince many that the once pagan king was not, despite appearance, so rough and uncultured that he was incapable of appreciating the fineness of Jadwiga's character, and that she suffered much because of this. All knew that their tastes were congenially simple, that Jagiello cared no more for wealth or possessions than the queen, that they were mutually abstemious and were on two days of the week eating little more than bread and water. They knew, too, that they were constantly conferring together over the many important and the lesser policies of their rule, and that hourly the king was entering farther into the queen's Christian world. Yet this was not enough. People persisted in their questioning. Were they really happy together? How could they be?

How could roughness and elegance, eastern and western culture, be so quickly harmonized? They set the exquisiteness of Jadwiga's personal appearance against that of her husband, who preferred going about the chateau in a Russian blouse and heavy casque—rarely had he accorded Henry, his tailor, the joy of making him a costume after the popular French mode. Did the queen condone the periods of passivity, almost of indolence, which followed the long and violent hunts which were his passionate pleasure? But while people questioned critically, they remembered the Lithuanian's modesty, his generosity, and the way in which he lived up to his promises. Frankly, they could not read him clearly. His seemed a strong nature, oscillating between control and uncontrol. He was a keen statesman, a trained man of the oriental diplomatic school, and yet at times he appeared to be as naïve as a peasant, a neophyte not only in religion, but in politics as well. But her subjects recognized that though the queen's days inside the circumference of her marital relationship might be drear, yet always above their grayness planed great-winged, bright-winged birds—her ideas, her hopes for her people.

Then something occurred which confirmed the

doubts of the pessimists. In those days intrigue was so much the breath of courtiers that even this devout couple could not escape the calumniator. Before they had been married a year, the master of the court, Gneawosz, was at work, simultaneously whispering to Jagiello that among the throng of visiting poets was William, whom Jadwiga had several times secretly received, and to Jadwiga that Jagiello was unfaithful to her.

And he proceeded so cleverly that after a time both apparently believed him. As did others outside. Even before this, there had been rumors of William's return; he was supposed to have come back incognito and for some time visited secretly his merchant friend, Count Morstin, in a castle near Krakow. In the mind of the people the earlier relationship was, through heroic renunciation, covered over; it could not die. They had seen a love they believed imperishable, and this conviction was fertile soil for the growth of romantic conjecture. The intriguer counted on it when he spread his reports.

Unhappy weeks! Jadwiga was hurt to the quick. Elizabeth, Constance, her loyal women, tried to defend her from her own thoughts. Fighting as she was to keep William even out of her mind, and to fail in no part of her great resolve, Jagiello's distrust of her threw her into proud revolt. She shut herself away from him, refusing to allow him to approach her. Once, when during confession, a priest urged her to admit him, she quickly and angrily left the confessional. The situation was growing constantly more strained when one day the council of the crown, which had been racking its brains to find some road toward reconciliation, proposed that both sovereigns reveal publicly the names of their informants. This they agreed to do, and instantly the intrigue was uncovered—whereupon not only the queen but the king and an outraged public turned upon Gneawosz. By their condemnation of him, and by their recognition of Jadwiga's innocence, the people felt the affair liquidated. But she had been too deeply wounded to let the matter rest there. She was not only queen but a woman, and now she demanded to be tried like any other woman. In court, before the world, she would win justification.

In such a case a woman was allowed to swear to her innocence and then send her representative to the trial, which Jadwiga did—her father's and her own loyal friend, the chatelain Jasko de Tenczyn, went to stand for her. He took with him twelve witnesses to her innocence and also twelve knights in armor ready to seek a true verdict by fighting against Gneawosz. But the trial collapsed at the start, for when the accused was questioned he was too overcome to utter a word in his own defense. He was, then, guilty and according to the law, must admit that he had lied like a dog, and pay a fine of sixty pieces of silver money. This penalty, however, did not satisfy; people demanded that in addition he be made to howl three times like the dog he was—and this also he did from beneath Jadwiga's royal chair. Thus peace was restored in the chateau. At least, restored outwardly, for despite the Christian rule of forgiveness, only time could heal Jadwiga's hurt.

King and queen sorely needed quiet on Wawel Hill. Jagiello's journey to Lithuania had but superficially ended dissensions there; though his half brother André, whose attempted usurpation had given him so much trouble during this year, was now a prisoner in Poland. To Skirgiello, on whom he depended most to quench such fires of disloyalty, he sent an extraordinary communication: "God has given us much," he wrote, "and therefore have I with my brother Skirgiello taken faith and intend to remain true. First, I promise my brother that he shall keep all the holdings which he now possesses; in particular, the principality of Troki, which I pledge myself never in anger or hate to deflect from him. Never will I listen to nor believe in evil tales of him told by bad people, but will acquaint him with everything, without concealment, good or bad. I will hold him higher and listen more to him than to all other friends and brothers. Him and his will I treat justly and not anger them, and punish all who ill-treat them, whether brother or half-brother."

Poland itself was still divided; even Krakow, which had supplanted Gnezno as capital when Galicia was first acquired, was not yet securely established as first city. And now, soon after she had triumphed in the trial and the trouble-maker had been dealt with, Jadwiga issued a decree which was of great importance in the struggle toward unity. It further defined and strengthened Jagiello's position, and shed fresh light on the character of the joint rule. In this decree, issued in December, 1387, she asked Krakow to swear to be just as loyal and obedient to him as to herself, and, should she die, to take him as king. Similar decrees were issued in other cities.

The nobles were restless; plots were hatching on all sides. And chiefly there was valorous but disturbing Prince Witowt to watch. In this early period he turned a favorable ear toward the White Capes. His desires did not stop with his visioned control of Lithuania, but included fantastic hopes of conquest in Russ, Tatar-held, lands. There seemed to be little hope that he and Jagiello could ever arrive at any such working agreement as the famous pact which existed between their fathers, Olgierd and Kiejstut, Jadwiga, as well as Jagiello, watched his expanding power with growing concern, though at times viewing it from different angles.

Jadwiga saw him draining Poland of supplies and money for his vast and questionable enterprise. Where would he stop? What dangers to the Poland of her father and Casimir lay in his dream of conquest in the east? As for Jagiello, though he envisaged a more extended Poland than she, he was at the same time ready to sacrifice every other consideration to the necessity of welding the Slavs into a thoroughly unified state, which would be a beneficent power in the middle of Christian Europe.

Yet Fate had assigned him a double rôle. Not only was he to develop a Slavic state strong enough to withstand the German pressure eastward; but by a dramatic reversal in history, the former pagan found himself standing as a defender of Europe against the two most powerful pagan forces in the world, the Golden Horde of Kipchak on whom Witowt's chivalric zeal was centered, and the Osman Turks. He must work, therefore, with Witowt, and yet restrain him. Already he was being drawn into a religious war which was to darken three centuries and would end victoriously only at the gates of Vienna.

The queen had an extraordinary relationship with both, in this drama of opposition and reconciliation enacted by Jagiello and Witowt. Her reputation for wisdom and fairness had grown steadily, until people from far away were coming to seek her advice. And more and more Jagiello and Witowt turned to her in their conflicts of ambition and judgment. Intensely moving is the picture of this young woman, so utterly free of self-interest, so completely dedicated to high and holy tasks, set between these two men, both willing to accept her judgment where each rejected the other's. As for herself, when she needed the advice of someone outside her immediate group of counsellors, she frequently consulted Jagiello's brother, Skirgiello, who had become increasingly her friend and confidant.

CHAPTER XX

Pacifism and Diplomacy

Jadwiga had acted decisively and courageously in the matter of the Ruthenian lands. She was firm in her attitude towards Prince Witowt's increasingly extravagant demands for money and troops and supplies for his eastern adventures. But in both these matters it was easy for her to chart her course compared with the difficulty of seeing a clear path in her relationship with the Order of Teutonic Knights. In their ambition lay Poland's greatest danger.

Their Golden Period was waning, though they believed it had only begun. From Marienburg, military headquarters, seat of learning, center of commerce and agriculture, administrative post for conquered territories counting two million inhabitants—largely German colonists whom they had settled there—the White Capes still rode forth to devastate and to acquire. That the Lithuanian was converted and his vast possessions joined, through a door of his own opening, with the western Christian world, this they refused to accept. They pressed more and more frankly now toward their true objective. They pictured themselves as an ever-growing state carrying civilization into regions of barbarism. Their effort had become, in fact, the increasingly threatening embodiment of the age-long *Drang nach Osten* which Poland blocked on the Vistula just as Lithuania held it at the Niemen.

Jagiello had been born into the life and death struggle of his country with the Order. Lithuanian captives had helped lift its walls and towers. At the mention of its name his hand was on his sword. He watched for the day when he could throw the combined strength of Poland and Lithuania against it; and end for long, if not for all time, that fear focussed on the towered and battlemented red brick citadel on the Vistula delta. Yet experience had taught that he must move with supreme adroitness.

Jadwiga's position was not so simple. As Queen of Poland, she, too, recognized in the Order her country's chief danger. But she had been brought up from childhood to see in the White Capes a holy brotherhood who were seeking to bring compensation to Christ and the Church in the north for losses to the infidel Turks of the south. How could she forget that one of the most prized episodes in her father's illustrious career had been his participation with these brothers in a crusade against the Saracens of the North; forget that his treasured sword hung in the hall at Marienburg? "Oh, if King Louis were still living!" their leader is said to have exclaimed. "Our well-wishing Seigneur on all occasions, our Defender at all times when we needed protection; we pray day and night for his soul."

She could still hear William's uncle dwelling with Christian satisfaction on his own co-operation in a crusade. The priests of her father's court, the chevalier-poet Suchenwirt and other singers and narrators who had been her teachers, had set a crown of glory above the Order's zeal. Thus it still held for her a deeply religious significance. At times she felt herself trapped in some impossible contradiction, living, as she did, with a husband but recently a pagan, and having to fight against the knights who wore emblazoned on their capes the cross of Christ. She struggled to reconcile these deep-seated impressions of the past with her knowledge of present reality. Furthermore, in a brutally warring century, she was by instinct and by young conviction a pacifist. She had a natural horror of battle and of all shedding of blood.

This necessity of reaching a sound policy toward the Order was the most difficult, the most important duty which, as queen, she faced. And the way in which she met it of itself lifted her to the level of greatness. The Order must be driven safely beyond all Polish-Lithuanian frontiers, Polish-Lithuanian objectives must be secured against any encroachment. But this must be accomplished not by fighting, but by negotiation. Her faith was so strong that she believed she could succeed, despite the sword-brandishing spirit of her age. And so, using all her influence to win Jagiello's support, she embarked on a course of persistent, patient and unwearying effort for a peaceful solution of an international difficulty which can bear comparison with any similar undertaking of our own time. Indeed, her diplomatic struggle to bring the Order to reason and justice was to stand as one of the extraordinary episodes of European history.

Again and again, in critical moments, she handled thorny negotiations, treating directly, in intimate conversation, with the grand master and influential leaders of this powerful organization; returning always with some kind of an arrangement; often, to be sure, unsatisfactory in itself but yet sufficient to prevent armed conflict. Nor did she allow her desire to win by pacific means deceive her, she knew well that war loomed darkly on the horizon. Folded away in the chronicles of the Order were occasional little notes written without Jagiello's knowledge, warnings of the inevitable break if they persisted "in angering my well-beloved husband."

An amazing picture! From the gates of Marienburg on the Nogat, the army of the White Capes, the helmets tufted with peacocks' feathers, the flashing swords, the accompanying hosts of archers—bear out upon the eastward road. And before them, attempting to block that road, stands the girl from Buda, the young Queen of Krakow, daughter of their former defender, her blue eyes shining with spiritual and patriotic purpose. . . .

She could not prevent the climax toward which the drama was moving, but as long as she lived, by vigilant and incessant intervention she succeeded in postponing that ineluctable conflict destined before long to make famous the field of Tannenburg five centuries before the campaign of Hindenburg.

Big issues drew Jadwiga's mind away from lesser griefs. She forgot her personal hurt caused by the court scandal and Jagiello's doubt of her. She also dismissed all estrangement or difficulty in their relations born of her pacifist diplomacy—and some asserted that there was serious estrangement. The meetings of the joint sovereigns were now increasingly important, and their deliberations ever more momentous. They had, from the beginning, agreed that matters of internal administration were particularly the king's responsibility, and international relations the queen's. And in general they followed this division of direction; though obviously there must be constant overlapping, for their discussions covered all fields.

While they were working out problems of war and peace with east and west, and of internal consolidation, they gave themselves together to the increasingly arduous social responsibilities of Wawel chateau. And concomitantly they carried forward their chosen task of beautifying not only the capital outspread below, but also that other far away capital, Vilno.

In this last decade of 1300, Krakow was starred on the traveller's parchment. Imagination kindled at the thought of the young queen, daughter of that great Anjevin, Louis of Hungary, who in her woman's frailty had accomplished far more for Christ than ever Louis had. People wanted to see with their own eyes the living picture of the most beautiful, wise and Christian queen of the Slav world yoked with the one-time pagan outcast, now given by the Pope "first place amongst all the kings of the earth in the affections of the Church." They wanted to see the miracle of this joint rule in operation. So they headed their cavalcades toward Krakow. As they journeyed they gathered news, both fact and rumor, so that arrivals were welcomed as the morning papers are today. One of the most interesting reports to reach the chateau during this last year before the last decade of 1300 was that the priest, John of Hess, while visiting the Holy Land had actually seen a unicorn and watched him at his water conning.

This romantic interest in Poland's capital meant an almost continuous series of receptions, banquets and tourneys on Wawel Hill, as it meant the housing and feeding in the city below of great numbers of knights and attendants accompanying princely visitors. In addition there were repeated family visits and celebrations; the influx of guests from the new Polish-Lithuanian Kingdom kept the Wawel chambers filled. Jagiello's brother Wigund, who, because of his wit and charm, was a great favorite at the Polish Court, had become engaged to the Duke of Oppeln's daughter, Jadwiga. The queen herself had gone with Oppeln to Niepolmice to celebrate the engagement, Jagiello joining them there on his way home from Vilno. During the two years preceding their marriage this popular couple were often fêted on the royal hill.

No guests were more frequently and more warmly welcomed than Duke Ziemovit and Duchess Alexandra, Jagiello's sister, who had become Jadwiga's intimate counsellor and friend. Jagiello was never so happy as when Alexandra was with him. He showered her with gifts—jewels, stuffs, horses—and in a myriad ways expressed an affection which was the strongest in his life. With her he felt inhibitions melt away. He could be his true self, unembarrassed by the fact that he still at times wore the bracelet of bison's hide inscribed with runic letters without which his old zest for the chase would, somehow, have suffered. He could feel comfortable about the Lithuanian hunters and valets he had brought down to accompany him on the chase, and about the Ruthenian cymbal and lute players whom he preferred, and unembarrassed by the many little cherished habits which bound him to their mutual past.

Friendships had sprung up, too, between members of the Mazovian suites and the Wawel courtiers, so that the whole hill looked forward to the visits of Ziemowit and the king's sister. When they came, according to custom, Jagiello entertained Ziemowit and Jadwiga, Alexandra.

On these occasions the great courtyard was alive with preparatory goings and comings. Extra wax was purchased so that the customary candlelight could be augmented by hundreds of additional gala tapers.

Fanfares of welcoming trumpets greeted the most powerful Duke and Duchess of the realm and their long following of knights as they rode through the lower gate. After the gleaming, clanking line had wound up around the hill, Duchess Alexandra and her women were escorted to their apartments near the queen's, and Duke Ziemowit and his knights to others farther away. There were informal exchanges of family news; then a drive to inspect a newly founded convent or church, or some other outing or ceremony pleasantly filled the late morning hours before dinner, which was served at two o'clock. At this function, as one elaborate course succeeded another, musicians and entertainers outdid themselves.

The women's banquets fell nothing short of the men's. The supplies which poured into both kitchens were so carefully recorded that we can easily today follow on the pages five hundred years old their clear notation. Often as many as ten dishes were served as one course, each person choosing from them those he preferred. For a single banquet, in honor of Ziemowit, Jagiello's chefs prepared one large and eight small pigs, sixty-two chickens, sixteen fat capons, sixteen geese, sixteen partridges, white turnips and beets and other vegetables, and used four pounds of butter and sixty pieces of cheese and one hundred eggs in preparing the popular cheese cakes of the time. To these offerings were added many skins of wine, kegs of beer, and large quantities of hydromel—people usually made their beer at home, but the court procured its supply from Krakow.

And on this same day Jadwiga's chefs cooked for herself and Alexandra and their company two fat cows, two hams, sixty chickens, seven well-larded hares, eight partridges, seven small pigs, quantities of turnips, carrots and beets, and used two hundred eggs, twelve cheeses, several pounds of butter, rice and mixed meal in the preparation of cakes and other dainties. For her tables as well as for the king's, there was both white and dark bread.

Something was always especially provided for the court poor,—on this occasion, among other things, six hams, fifteen chickens and a great number of slices of dark bread. And the overbusy kitchens were at the same time giving thought to merchants and agents and other travellers—seeing, for instance, that the men who had brought one hundred dogs from England for the king and queen were being properly fed.

Occasionally the sovereigns themselves enjoyed the variety of dining out. Royal custom did not bar their acceptance of certain invitations, those for instance, of the bishop, or of important officers of state. At these times, combining business with pleasure, they discussed governmental problems with their hosts. And so the full days passed.

Small wonder that people were attracted by Wawel hospitality and fascinated by the kaleidoscopic shifting of the spectacle within its encircling walls and tree greenery. From whichever angle they viewed this particular scene on the world stage, its brilliant aspects appeared yearly heightened, as the tremendous potentialities of the Polish-Lithuanian union stood more clearly revealed.

Thus, as the twilight of the century fell, Jadwiga found her days surcharged. She was now a mature queen approaching twenty! Sufficiently overwhelming within earlier boundaries would have been her royal duties and aspirations. But now she was setting the objectives for a realm so far-flung that she could but vaguely picture its frontiers. Moreover, when she gave up William and took Jagiello, she, who did nothing by halves, added to her responsibilities, not only those Lithuanian cares which directly concerned Poland, but throwing heart and brain into the enlarged situation, she shared her husband's every anxiety concerning his former country and its people. His multiple family difficulties troubled her more than those of her own pitifully diminished family, though she kept in as close touch as she could with her sister Mary, now ruling with Sigismund at Buda.

To internal difficulties was added again during the last year of this decade the imminent danger of invasion. The Osman Turks had pressed as far as Kossovo, where in a fatal battle they sounded the knell of Servia. Where would they next advance? Sigismund and Mary were turning for help to the Christian states of western Europe.

CHAPTER XXI

ARBITRESS

As 1390 got under way, Jagiello was desperately engaged in trying to prevent old enemies without and warring members of his family inside Lithuania's boundaries, from undoing what he had accomplished in the past few years. In the east, Russ princes were continually plotting to make the most of his increased preoccupation with affairs of the united kingdom; in the west the Order watched. No sooner did his ambitious brothers seem more or less satisfied with lands and positions allotted them, than one among them by some covetous act broke the precarious peace, thus furnishing the opportunity the outside foe waited to seize.

It would have been far easier to control these brothers had it not been for the ever disturbing presence of their more clever, more ambitious cousin, Prince Witowt, who aimed at nothing less than the mastery of Vilno. Witowt particularly resented Skirgiello's hold on the beautiful Lake Troki lands, once the favorite property of his father Kiejstut. He objected, indeed, to all of this cousin's advance in power, an advance deliberately designed by Jagiello to check his own. The two were ready to fly at each other's throats. "Beware of me, as I of you," Skirgiello had sent him word by his servant Marfz. Had the king not been born in an atmosphere of turbulence and had he been less a believer in his fortunate star, he might have despaired over this situation.

Early in 1390 the Order, reversing its policy, decided to invade Lithuania during the summer. Henry of England (who was to become Henry IV) arrived with three hundred archers to join in the attack, along with Knight Boucicault of France, and men from Livland and others. Witowt led the heathen Samogitians, to whom with rare irony, the Order guaranteed freedom in the practice of their pagan religion as a reward for aid in this war against now Christian Lithuanians! By September the formidable force arrived before Vilno and began a combined siege of the capital. It was a terrible year. Toward its close Jagiello was forced to hurry north with a Polish army to retake castles captured by Witowt. Witowt's brother was killed, but he himself escaped to Prussia, only to return in '91 and again with the Order as ally to lay siege to Vilno. This attempt was one of the bloodiest ever witnessed in a land inured to sanguinary warfare; the breaches in the walls surrounding the chateau were filled with corpses. To intimidate its defenders, the head of Jagiello's brother Casimir was lifted on a pick before them. But in the end both Witowt and the Order learned once again that the king's arm was stronger than their own. Yet in the new year, the Order recrossed the Lithuanian border and destroyed the city of Grodno.

The death of several of her sons and strife amongst others caused Jagiello's mother, Julianna, such grief that when early in the decade, she died, it was in bitter pain over their hard fate.

These rebellions and invasions troubled Jagiello not only as demonstrations of the yet divided state of his kingdom, but also because they destroyed so much that he had ardently undertaken. One of the most moving aspects of his activity as western Christian king was his effort to carry to his northern people as quickly as possible the best that he found in the south. He had given them the Christian religion and their Charter. Since then he had been trying to turn the potential benefits of these gifts into experienced realities.

Converts had to be kept in line. The powerful pagan priesthood, resisting desperately, were still, in the endless forests, offering sacrifices to the old gods. It was to be expected that many Lithuanians were but externally converted. One does not doff and don his religion as he does his cloak. "The Prince ordered it," the puzzled neophyte said, "so I prostrate myself before the Christ. But surely I am not obliged to deprive our ancient devils of the crumbs of my cheese or the foam of my beer or a roasted turnip? If they are discontented my horses will break, calves catch the mange, my cows give blood instead of milk, my harvest rot where it stands." For some time old beliefs would follow secretly close beside the new. Only step by step could the people truly be brought to Christ, just as only degree by degree could they truly win the liberties bestowed on them by the Charter.

Jagiello was impatient to see wide-spreading Vilno beside the Vilyia transformed to a city of brick that could rank proudly with others. Where was another more beautifully environed by rolling wooded lands and shining lakes? He was continually planning for the new Christian capital he pictured. And in all of this planning Jadwiga was his chief encourager and aid.

He had begun the Cathedral of Saint Stanislaus, and among others, the fine churches of Saint John and Saint Martin, and was busy with projects for monasteries and hospitals, when these desolating wars cut across progress. In 1390 he wrote the Pope that the Order had not only burned practically all of Vilno (the ducal chateau on the hilltop had been saved by Polish soldiers arrived in the nick of time) but that they had also deliberately destroyed a splendid church he was building and used the material to throw a bridge across the Vilyia.

Jadwiga felt as deeply as he the loss of this church. For months needles had been stitching and knotting that it should lack no accessories. The Polish-Lithuanian court was one of the busiest in Europe. Jagiello never journeyed north without taking with him gifts of beautiful embroideries and other ornaments.

Clearly, if Lithuania was to develop into a healthy member of the family of western nations, there must be an end to invasion and rebellion. Before all else there must be an end to the enmity between Witowt and Skirgiello who was so strongly favored by Jagiello. Jadwiga had long hoped and worked for a reconciliation. Many influential persons outside were endeavoring, too, to bring it about, chief among them the picturesque young Bishop Henry of Plock, half-brother of Duke Ziemowit, who had a much greater flair for diplomatic than for ecclesiastical enterprise. When, earlier, Jagiello had sent him on a secret mission to Witowt he fell head over heels in love with Witowt's attractive sister, Ryngalla, and throwing the celibacy rule to the winds, had married her! His career as married bishop formed one of the most romantic episodes of this romance-charged period.

It was skillful Bishop Henry, then, who arranged with Jagiello's rebellious cousin that he should meet the king somewhere between Krakow and Vilno to adjust these differences which threatened the very life of the kingdom. They chose as the conference center a Lithuanian chateau at Ostrow, in Russ-Lithuanian territory south of Vilno, near the river Ditwa. Bishop Henry dispatched the cheering word to Krakow. The members of Jagiello's family so greatly admired Jadwiga and had such confidence in her wisdom and fairness, that the best pledge for the successful outcome of this meeting at Ostrow would be her presence there.

So both the king and the queen made hurried preparations for the northeastward journey. They would have preferred not to be absent at the same time and for so long, but unquestionably they must go. The council of the crown and the two courts co-operated in every way to facilitate their departure. Among them were a few who remembered the time when King Louis with a flashing army had travelled in a similar direction to make war on the pagan wolf and his idolatrous people. Now his daughter was to ride forth with that "Wolf" on a peace mission to Lithuania. They shut their eyes—these reversals were staggering.

How lifted above all others she was, this twenty year old queen of theirs—where in Europe was her equal? With all her loveliness of thick, silky hair and fresh-hued skin, and deep blue eyes, her expression bespoke a masculine firmness and decision which augmented a royal dignity. Good will and holiness shone from her face. There was reverence and true affection in the handwavings and goodbyes that sent her north. And proud loyalty in the bearing of those who escorted her.

It was the magical season of the year. The state coach and the wagons and horses clattered down Wawel Hillside between flanking trees flecked with scarlet and gold. Overhead a light fleece of mackerel clouds floated against the distant blue. Asters and late roses bloomed in the bordering plots. About the villages beyond the capital spread rippling seas of heavy-headed rye and wheat; orchards were sweet with apples. It would have been pleasant to give oneself to free enjoyment of the late summer landscape. But there could be no loitering—with anxious thoughts king and queen pressed forward, and by early August were within the Lithuanian boundary. Now the forest stretches on either side of them were dark with fir and pine, and peopled by bear and wolves. In the towns Christian spires gave way to the rounded cupolas of the Greek Orthodox Church.

Everywhere the coming of the holy Jadwiga awakened profound emotion. People crowded to see her and to kneel as she passed, as if she were a saint arrived from the still more or less vague but glorious western world. They held their sick children up to her, for had they not heard of the beggar covered with sores, neglected by all others, whom she had washed with her own hands until a light shone in the dark corner and he rose, healed?

In Ostrow one might have been in the middle of Russia. Buildings and costumes were completely oriental. The women who crowded the streets with the men wore heavily embroidered short coats, full woolen skirts and boots, and on almost all their fingers rings of one metal or another. Some of the women were blue-eyed and white-throated, others had dark eyes and braids wound coronal wise. They knelt as they cheered, and lifted their hands to the holy queen.

She smiled her assent. Yes, she would visit their sick and their miserable, once the business of state was finished.

The castle, set in spreading, heavy-scented gardens, was handsomely built and comfortably appointed. In the long meeting chamber decorated with barbaric splendor, the group of hunters and warriors assembled; clad now in embroidered velvets and fine furs and jewelled ornaments, and accompanied by their wives whose robes would have shone in any court of the East. Foremost among the women was Anna, Witowt's clever and vivacious wife.

Jadwiga had always felt as if a strong wind had blown into the room when these men of the north appeared—today they suggested a hurricane. The four near walls seemed to stretch to the earth's frontiers as these adventurers who lived in their saddles in black forests and on perilous steppes, where a poisoned arrow or a death fall from a madly racing horse awaited one after the other, gathered about her.

The discussions were long, at times angry, then calmer. But as each memorable day closed, it showed more clearly than the preceding the confidence of all in the justice of the queen. And in the end Witowt and Jagiello were reconciled. Witowt swore loyalty to the king, who promised to raise his title and to turn over to him the lands once held by his father Kiejstut. Anna pledged herself as security that her husband would live up to his promise. There seemed now to be definite hope of peace.

On August 4, 1392, this first agreement was solemnly recorded. Witowt expressed his joy over the ending of old and bloody quarrels and vowed to remain eternally loyal to the Polish Kingdom, Polish crown and the Polish Queen Jadwiga, adding that he would never know any sovereign other than herself but on the contrary would contribute all his strength to her worship, benefit, power and glory, as well as defend, protect and shelter her from all enemies and opponents.

But when Skirgiello, who in compensation for the loss of the Troki lands had been given others about the many-templed city of Kiev, heard that his brother had made such an arrangement without first consulting him (as he had agreed to do) he was filled with anger. As were the other brothers who saw their position threatened. Imitating their cousin's earlier practice, they appealed to the ever-ready Order to aid them in fighting to prevent the fulfillment of Jagiello's agreement with Witowt. Thus things appeared worse than before.

The royal pair had returned to Krakow believing that the Lithuanian situation was well in hand. But every courier from the north brought black news. Jagiello's brother Wigund, very dear to him, had died of poison—another warning that he himself must not abate his vigilance. Then came word of Skirgiello's opposition, with the report that trouble had broken out afresh among all the brothers.

The king and queen faced this recurrent disruption with profound disquiet. However, Jadwiga's faith in the eventual success of conference and arbitration was undaunted. Another meeting must be arranged with all speed; with Witowt and Skirgiello together at Ostrow, some agreement could be worked out. Again couriers flew back and forth across the Polish-Lithuanian border. And then again the sovereigns set out, travelling by relays, and reaching Ostrow in record time.

In the crucial days which followed, Jadwiga's faith splendidly triumphed. The cousins were reconciled, and Witowt wrote a letter recording the fact that he and Skirgiello had in her presence adjusted their differences.

Furthermore, again rendering homage to her wisdom and magnanimity, the members of Jagiello's family agreed that in all future disagreements which might arise amongst them Queen Jadwiga should be asked to arbitrate. A new period of settlement by arbitration with Jadwiga as Arbitress, had begun. Five documents registered the conciliatory steps by which the final broad agreement was reached.

The little girl, who with her boy lover, beside the Danube had listened shiveringly to tales of the heathen of the dark north, now as queen accepted this extraordinary investiture. Her own sense of usefulness and power were a balm to her great hurt—heaven which denied her a child, still vouchsafed approval in other ways.

CHAPTER XXII

Lifting the Torch

In her rôle as arbitress, Queen Jadwiga was not often to be appealed to by her friend Skirgiello. At the close of the very year following the family councils he died near Kiev. Rumor said of poison, dropped into his beaker by a monk of Orthodox faith who had heard that the Lithuanian had decided to enter the western Church and was planning a pilgrimage to Rome. When Skirgiello fell ill a call for a physician was sent to Krakow, but though Doctor Dominic set out in all haste, he reached Kiev too late. The death of his brother was a severe blow for Jagiello. Of all the family, he had always been nearest, and troublesome though he at times was, he had yet been the king's strongest support on Lithuanian soil. With the passing of Skirgiello, the three most powerful of Jagiello's brothers were out of Witowt's way.

And now Jadwiga had to turn her thoughts to her own family. Her brother-in-law, King Sigismund, was coming to the Polish-Hungarian frontier to arrange new treaties covering the Russian provinces and other matters. She was elated, for this visit meant direct news of Mary and of friends and loved places. She gathered together beautiful gifts for her sister and for old teachers and companions, and with a large following started toward the Carpathians to meet the approaching visitors. In a castle near her southern border she welcomed Sigismund, and then as the red and white stripes of the Árpáds and the Slavic white eagle on a red field floated over them, Hungarians and Poles proceeded together to Sandec. There the visit was royally celebrated while the diplomatic discussions advanced to a satisfactory conclusion. When Jadwiga returned to Krakow she carried with her, happily, Sigismund's promise that during the very first month of the new year he would bring Mary to Poland for her long-delayed visit.

As we watch the queen journeying first to one frontier, then to another, back and forth between her capital and those of the provinces, from city to city, in barges or in springless carriages and on horseback over the roads of her day, we wonder how she did much more than prepare for and recuperate from these taxing excursions. Just as, when realizing her preoccupation with the international relations of the new empire, we ask how she crowded into the days her myriad more immediate undertakings.

Yet she seemed continually engaged in establishing new hospitals and schools, monasteries, convents and churches, and in enlarging old establishments. She bestowed and reaffirmed privileges and grants—among them often those of yearly salt from the famous mines—inspected and encouraged one institution after another. She visited the sick and otherwise unfortunate untiringly, and listened to appeals for justice and mercy, even from men and women from beyond her borders; for belief in her goodness and power intensified and spread.

She had particularly filled with good works the year 1390, declared a holy year by Pope Boniface IX. She increased during this time her hours of meditation and study of the Church fathers and saints, among whom Saints Ambrose and Bernard and Bridget and Catherine continued to be her favorites. She added, also, more days of self-denial; though already she and Jagiello limited themselves two days a week to bread and water. At certain seasons, as during the pre-Easter period, she dressed almost as a nun, wearing a dark veil and a rough garment next to her skin. Many felt that they saw in this the influence of her ancestor Saint Louis, who a hundred years earlier had worn a hair shirt and had carried chains for flagellation about with him in an ivory box. Indeed, remembering the reports that King Louis had wanted, toward the end of his life, to enter a monastery, they would not have been surprised to hear that his daughter had decided to renounce the world altogether. Throughout the Jubilee year, Poland was bidding godspeed to the many pilgrim bands starting for the Holy City; and Jadwiga envied those free to go.

It was at this time, shortly after the completion of the Convent of the Visitation near Krakow Gate, that she and Jagiello called Benedictines from Prague to found an abbey near Kleparz, where in their

Church of the Holy Cross the daily service would be recited in the Slavic language. And in other foundations she now insisted that at least at certain seasons both mass and song should be rendered in Slavic. She was an enthusiast in church music and did much to improve the singing, not only in Krakow Cathedral, where she encouraged the introduction of psalms of David chanted in two parts by seventeen voices, but in other churches as well.

Consciously and unconsciously she was making her own important contribution to the reform movement that was sweeping across Europe. Wickliffe had died the year after her coronation; in England Lollardism was well under way, and to the south of her, John Huss, her own age, was receiving degrees from Prague university. But while following the democratic tendencies of the reform movement, by her unswerving loyalty to the Church, she was helping to keep the Polish branch safe from the extreme of separation. In other countries the disrepute into which the papacy had fallen during the great schism, and the suffering resulting from simony and other extortions, prepared the soil for rebellion. But in Poland the effect of such evils was gloriously counteracted by the spirit of exaltation in which the country had witnessed the conversion of the last pagan people of western Europe, and in which it looked to further triumphs for the Cross in the east. Why could not all Slav peoples be united through the western Church? In this part of the world the "Victory of Jadwiga" was still vividly present in all minds, and the Church, despite its mistakes, was a living, growing body. There was freedom of opinion and speech, the new doctrines were reported and discussed, while the holy queen and her people worked with increased zeal inside the fold.

During five hundred years Poland has been reverently grateful to Jadwiga for her effort to bring religion and learning within the reach of all; and for being, as she was, one of the first to appreciate the beauty and importance of the Slavic language, and through her unwearying insistence on its use inside and outside the Church, helping to insure to her country its share in the fructifying influences of the rise of vernacular languages. Not only the translation of the scriptures, which she ordered, but many other translations due to her, added to the riches of the Polish tongue. Nothing could have won her warmer co-operation than the knowledge that she was writing in her own hand a translation of the greater part of the New Testament. In these and many other ways she gave impetus to the Polish renaissance.

It was not surprising that Pope Boniface IX, who deeply appreciated her great qualities, should write her a letter (in 1390) in which he thanked her for her devotion to the Catholic Church, adding that though it was impossible to accede to all applications transmitted to the See on behalf of her subjects, yet if she adopted a confidential sign manual for those requests to which she personally attached importance, they would be immediately granted. In another letter this pontiff gently complained that she sometimes recommended people contrary to her conviction because she could not refuse a favor!

To the two dominant forces of this century, those of the empire and the Church, had been added a third, that of the university. At the side of empire and Church, the university was to play a rôle of incalculable importance in the march of human destiny. The Holy See knew and approved of Queen Jadwiga's determination to give Krakow the thoroughly grounded university which Casimir had attempted, but failed to establish. The University of Prague was flourishing; she herself had opened there in connection with it a school of theology for Poles. Padua, Bologna, Paris, had long attracted Polish students; Heidelberg, but a few years old, was growing rapidly. Why should not Krakow furnish like opportunities to Poles and Lithuanians? Jadwiga decided to buy, one by one, through Jagiello's agent, Jewish houses along a street (now Saint Anne's) running off from the capital's harmonious market place, until an adequate site should be secured. In the year preceding her journey to Lithuania the first house had been bought.

Fortunately, the queen had men on whose experience and wise counsel she could draw to help make her university dream a reality. The learned Krakovian, Matthew, who had won the highest degree Prague could award, elaborated the plans with her. So interested was he, that after he had been made rector of Heidelberg University, he returned on leave to Krakow to devote himself to the Queen's project. Both Jadwiga and the city of Krakow showed appreciation of this patriotism by awarding him generous presents and honors.

Another inspiring aid was a Bohemian, the Cistercian, John Stekna, whom Jadwiga received often at Court. In fact both her own and Jagiello's court maintained intimate relations with Prague. John, who was a brilliant preacher, became her confessor and the executor and at times the instigator of her educational projects. Just as the learned Jerome of Prague became Jagiello's favorite preacher and confessor, and accompanied him everywhere, to the satisfaction of the Polish soldiers as well; for they particularly enjoyed his sermons.

However, in her planning and executing no one aided the queen more now than her revered and loved advisor, Peter Wysz, who, having received the degree of doctor of laws from Padua University, had been stationed in Krakow in '89 by Pope Urban VI, as papal nuncio and collector of papal incomes. He was a great friend of Elizabeth's husband, Spytko, which fact pleasantly strengthened the bond between him and his queen. In these days the bishop of Krakow had greater influence in politics than any other bishop in Poland, and when, in '93, Bishop John died, in spite of the fact that the Pope and the chapter had another candidate for the vacancy, Jadwiga forced through the election of Peter, then about forty-two years old. Thenceforth he accompanied her on nearly all of her missions and she rarely undertook anything of importance without consulting him.

She depended most upon him and upon Jasko of Tenczyn, who, as well, owed his position of chatelain of Krakow (the first secular dignity in the Polish state) to her influence. With Jasko, of course, the ties of friendship were older. Ever since her father had singled him out as quick, clever, and energetic, he had been one of the staunchest defenders of the Anjou dynasty. It was he who by his eloquent appeal at the meeting of Sieradz in '83, had turned the tide away from Ziemowit and saved the Polish throne for herself.

Queen Jadwiga would have preferred being able to concentrate all her efforts upon churches and schools and hospitals, not only in Poland proper but in Lithuania and the outlying Russ provinces, where the Benedictines whom she had sent to carry western civilization there were doing such excellent work. To ameliorate suffering, to give the joys of learning and religion to her subjects—these were her supreme desires. When, however, she had to turn from these nearest interests to other matters, she gave them her complete attention. One of the secrets of her power was her capacity to throw her whole energy into whatever she undertook.

Now it was the turn of the Teutonic Knights again to worry Wawel Hill. In midsummer of '94, Conrad von Jungingen, the new Master, declared a crusade against Lithuania, which stretched its bloody course into the autumn, ending only after Jagiello sent a Polish army to aid Witowt, who was valiantly trying to thrust back the onslaught of Conrad's army. This was the Order's last attempt against Vilno for a long time. Gradually world enthusiasm for these holy wars against a "pagan people" had been fading and contributions in money and men dwindling. In Europe's courts the new empire's prestige was steadily growing. When the diplomatic agents of Marienburg arrived, they found either Polish and Lithuanian representatives already there, or following close at their heels. Finally, in 1395—almost a decade after the great conversion!—King Wenceslaus of Bohemia ordered all crusades against Lithuania stopped.

In fact, Lithuania was acquiring a semblance of stability. Witowt had been learning from both Jagiello and Jadwiga that he could win more by a constructive use of his intellectual powers than by destructive warfare. He had recently declared himself a Catholic prince and was increasingly employing the method of peaceful negotiation and alliance.

Neither recurrence of intensified conflict with the Order nor rumblings of the approach of another heightened period of internal intrigue due to the perennial trouble makers, Dukes Wladislaus of Oppeln and Ziemowit of Mazovia, could drive from Jadwiga's mind the obsessing happy thought that the time of her sister's visit was almost at hand. Nor prevent her from giving personal attention to minutest details of the preparations for celebrating this event of the opening year—to her in many ways the dearest occasion of her reign.

Queen Mary was coming! Dressmakers and cooks, leatherers and jewellers, were feverishly busy. The quarters of horses and hounds and falcons echoed the general excitement. All sorts of gilded confections and little cakes sprinkled with poppy seed and mushroom sauces and other delicacies were piling up on the chefs' pantry shelves, while fine French and southern wines were being set aside in the deep Wawel cellars. The king like the queen had ordered splendid new garments for the visit, and had personally selected scores of beautiful presents for his brother-in-law's followers. Mary's chief gifts were a little book of the passion in an enamelled binding just arrived from Bruges, and a saddle covered with light brown velvet intricately patterned with yellow and brown silk, for which Jadwiga and the saddlemaker had devised a special padding.

The public, always eagerly curious concerning the gift-giving, which was as the color to the wine in all festivities, approved of the saddle, for next to a fine horse, the Pole coveted a fine saddle. They were following all preparations with live interest; throughout the land talk centered on the approaching reunion of the sisters. Many persons from the Hungarian quarter of the capital had applied, in one capacity or another, to travel with the royal procession to the border. And at court, the queen's dark-eyed friend

Elizabeth and others who had escorted her from Hungary and were now to return with her to the frontier of her homeland, were elated. The face of good bishop Peter radiated pleasure as he helped direct arrangements.

Quite aside from their enthusiastic anticipation of the meeting, fortunate persons who were to have a share in welcoming their Hungarian neighbors were thrilled at the prospect of a journey through the lovely Galician mountain lands in this shining January. Fir and pine boughs would be softly white, waterfalls crystal, skies deepest blue.

Everything progressed successfully, from the departure and the brilliant advance, often heightened by the welcome of carollers repeating for their majesties the Christmas songs that a few days earlier had echoed in the villages, to the settling in the border castle, the tumultuous welcome of the long cavalcade from the south, and the final embrace of the sisters. From vivid Jadwiga and gentle Mary down, no one tried to restrain or conceal his emotion.

The eight years difference in the ages of Louis' daughters showed less now than before. In fact Jadwiga's superior vitality and the impression she gave of power and poise, made her appear the more mature of the two. The crown had brought little joy to Mary.

Between formal gatherings they walked, arms interlaced, along the crisp paths of the castle gardens, pouring out questions that had been waiting so long for answers that cannot be written, exchanging news, happy and sad. Mary had to retrace, hour by hour, those desperate days of the fatal journey to Dalmatia and their mother's horrible death, and tell the story of her own ten months imprisonment. When they talked of mother and father, they drew closer—how alone they were!

Childless both! Many things they understood now which they had not even sensed at Buda and Visegrád—their grandmother Elizabeth's longing for sons for her son, their mother's chagrin and suffering, and the strength of their father's love which surmounted his own disappointment. And yet their mother had given him and the state daughters; the curse of barrenness had not been laid upon her as upon them—was it never to be lifted? What relief they found in releasing at last that pent-up pain and despair which they tried always to hide from others.

They discussed their husbands, as husbands, and as rulers. Hungary had not expected Mary to find happiness with Sigismund, nor had it counted on great benefits for itself through him. Ever since Louis' death, things had been going badly in his kingdom. For Mary as for Jadwiga happiness lay only in the rewards of piety and of patriotic devotion. How much they talked of girlhood experiences and friends, what Jadwiga's questions and Mary's reports about William might be, others could only divine. William had not married, that they knew.

The marvelous days passed swiftly. At the end it was inexpressibly difficult to turn again in opposite directions. One wonders if the sisters would have been able to do so, despite the inexorable forces controlling queens, could they have looked ahead but four short months. On the day of parting, Poles, with loud calls of good luck and lifting of pennants and hand-waving, followed their Hungarian friends as far as they could—the two queens were the last to stop waving.

The warmth and splendor of this border visit, demonstrating as it did the closeness of the ties binding Poland and Hungary, greatly heartened both peoples. Besides it had borne concrete results in renewed treaties.

CHAPTER XXIII

Tenth Anniversary

In May, Queen Mary died after a fall from a horse. The news was almost as great a shock to Poland as to Hungary. The heart of the people ached for the queen. She was, to be sure, acquainted with grief. Death seemed to stand at her elbow; but this sorrow would in many ways be hardest to bear. Desolate indeed she appeared; of the line of Charles Robert and Louis she alone remained.

Once again Jadwiga carried her trouble to the Blessed Virgin, whose ear was never so weary that she could not hear. She spent hours on her knees before the tall crucifix in the royal chapel, and before the Madonna above the prie-dieu in her chamber. There was something intimately comforting in this picture of the Madonna. It had been brought to her from Florence nine years ago, and ever since, the narrow space about it had havened her loved ones and had been her true home within the far-spreading chateau. She knew every fold of the Blessed Virgin's star-spangled blue robe and gauzy, pearl-edged headdress, every curve of the beautiful oval face with its compassionate brown eyes, and of the slender, speaking hands. Scribe John had many times told her and her sister, as they watched him in his workshop at Buda, that hands could express as much as a face. As she knelt she could often feel Mary's hand softly touch her bowed head. When not in prayer, she found much consolation in conversations with Bishop Peter; he was a tower of strength to her in these days.

Fortunately, she was obliged to give immediate attention to the question of whether or not she should claim the Hungarian crown, her legitimate heritage. This she determined to do. She resolutely took the title left by Queen Mary; though Jagiello, while conceding her right to do so, was opposed to any attempt to unite the two thrones. He saw a weakening, not a strengthening of the Slav Kingdom as a result of an extension southward. However, he led an army for the queen and her party beyond the Carpathians. On Hungarian soil it was soon proved that she had not sufficient support to succeed, and after making certain temporary agreements, the Poles withdrew peacefully across the border.

When later, Sigismund, who had been warring against the armies of the Sultan Bajazet, and had returned both beaten and robbed from the unlucky battle of Nicopolis, hurried to Krakow to seek aid, and assurance against any renewal of Jadwiga's attempt to claim the Árpád inheritance, he found, to his relief, a friendly reception. He was in sore need of encouragement. His splendid army, half of it Hungarian, had been practically wiped out by the Turks; southern Hungary, it seemed would soon become a desert. Troubles in Dalmatia, too, were growing. Since Mary's death there was no strong tie between the Hungarians and their restless, inconstant king. He knew that if he lacked security in the north, anything might happen. So it was with relief and renewed hope that he departed from the Wawel carrying a treaty guaranteeing a sixteen-year peace between the neighbor countries. And this, despite the fact that not very long before, he had been negotiating with the Teutonic Order the division of Poland, a fact which Jagiello was willing to overlook in his eagerness to prevent any rupture in those peaceful relationships in the west which he conceived to be the only sure foundation for the structure he was building.

Other important matters occupied the queen's thought—never from the beginning until the end of her life did she permit personal sorrow to interfere with state duties. Though she and the king had known less anxiety recently about Lithuania, they felt disquietude because of a flare-up in the Duke of Oppeln's quarter. He had seized several provinces, necessitating Jagiello's sending envoys to eject him from them by force. However, his picturesque career was nearing its close, already friends were deserting him. During half a century he had been struggling for independent control of ever larger territories; intrigues, pacts, dispatches had been his life. After his removal from the governorship of the Russian provinces for trying to hold the army in his own hands against the crown, he had received northern

Dobryzin lands. But it had not been possible for him to remain there, or in fact in Poland. He was often in Hungary fomenting a scheme to divide Poland, an intrigue in which, as usual, the Order was implicated. It was particularly painful to Jadwiga to see this earliest friend and supporter, now a constant source of disorder and danger. It was to Oppeln's protection that her mother had confided her, when she sent her, reluctantly and with misgiving, to Poland. And it was he who had boldly sponsored the happy meetings in the Franciscan refectory during William's visit in Krakow.

With the power of this disturber of the peace waning, royal watchfulness could focus on Ziemowit of Mazovia, whose ambition constituted an even stronger pull away from the centralization now under way. His marriage with Jagiello's sister Alexandra had helped to win a loyalty which the king through a policy of concession, was endeavoring to hold. But whenever this involved the ceding of purely Polish territory, Jagiello encountered the determined opposition of both his wife and the dominant nobles. As he did in '95, when after having planned to give Ziemowit Radom, he was finally persuaded to withdraw that offer and to substitute for it Belz and several other cities.

It was not surprising that Jagiello, who had brought with him to Poland no binding traditions and obligations concerning such crown possession, should fail to feel the same responsibility toward them that the grand niece of Casimir the Great and daughter of Louis the Great felt. From childhood she had been taught the importance of holding them intact. When only sixteen she had not needed the king's advice to make her set bravely forth at the head of an army to rescue the Ruthenian provinces. So far as Jagiello sought to give Poland more logical boundaries, she was in accord, but she was unalterably against alienation of any land whose loss might curtail the extent and the strength of the kingdom. She had always valued the Polish-Lithuanian union chiefly because of its religious significance and never thought of it as an obstacle to the performance of her first duty, that of preserving her inheritance from Casimir through her father, as he had left it to her.

She and the controlling group of magnates were against giving Belz to Ziemowit, as they had been against giving him Radom. But now they were not standing on equally sure ground; for though Belz had been won by Polish arms, a Lithuanian duke ruled it when Jagiello came to Poland. At this point, other troubles so engrossed the king that rather than risk more with Ziemovit, he carried through his arrangement with his brother-in-law, in spite of Jadwiga's opposition.

In '96, the nobles called a meeting in Krakow to consider Ziemowit's demands and to arrive at some agreement as to how best to protect crown lands. Among other things they decided that he should be given Volhynian territory, but Queen Jadwiga refused to confirm the grant until a year later. After she had done so, Ziemowit's payment in gold was deposited in her treasury, instead of the king's, to make it appear that she had contracted the sale! The subterfuge precipitated further difficulties which culminated in the paying back of the gold to Ziemowit and the return of lands which, along with those retaken from the Duke of Oppeln, were important in the rounding out of Poland's boundaries.

After this clash, the king added to the queen's income, from the revenues of the salt mines of Bochnia and Wieliczka two thousand marks a year, "that our dearest consort may be more comfortable and in better state"!

As with each year's added experience, Jadwiga's confidence in her own judgment grew, it was to be expected that king and queen would find increasing points of difference in their policies. They were often in opposition regarding their relations with the Order and with Prince Witowt, but it was over this question of crown lands that their divergence was perhaps widest.

However, in a conflict of opinion, whether with the king or the magnates, the queen usually won. All honored her intelligence, and the effect of her beauty and personality which had made Skirgiello and Witowt and their warring brothers trust their difficulties to her, was not waning, but increasing.

With the dawn of 1396 the royal differences appeared suddenly less serious. This year marked the close of the first decade of the double reign, and throughout the land it was with an intense feeling of satisfaction and gratitude that the people, taking stock, viewed the ten years just closing against those of the nightmare of the interregnum. How beneficent, in comparison, had been this period which restored what the preceding one had destroyed.

The Lithuanian had fulfilled to the letter his promises, and then thrown in something for fuller measure. He had demonstrated qualities of statesmanship, of foresightedness, which they had not thought he possessed. With what extraordinary swiftness this pagan of yesterday, this dreaded enemy of Poland, had assumed the responsibilities of a constitutional monarch! He had proved his capacity to assimilate western conceptions, as he pushed toward the goal of making the double kingdom an eminently European power in the service of civilization and Catholicism.

The resilient, imaginative Slavs love a festival; Krakow threw itself into preparations for the anniversary with unbounded zest. Whole forests of pine and fir branches seemed to be bearing in upon the capital, as, with jingling of bells and calling of fur-capped drivers, the laden sleds raced in and out through the gates. Bright city flags, the three square towers with Saints Stanislaus and Wenceslaus, and the nation's white eagle floated above the January snow. Rugs and tapestries hung from the windows of the burgher palaces flanking the market place; Saint Mary's Cathedral and other churches and outdoor shrines were ablaze with candles. Men and women in fur coats—some of rough goat or sheep, some of wolf or astrakan, poured into the city from all quarters of the kingdom. There was gay rivalry over the splendor of the painted sleds, the lines of the high-stepping horses, and the beauty of ribbons and tree boughs.

Many of the men who had gone ten years before to meet the Lithuanian, led in the celebrating. Dobieslaw, former castellan of Wawel chateau, and Archbishop Bodzanta of Gnezno, who had baptized and crowned him, were dead. But Jasko, Dimitri of Goray, Peter Kmita, Spytko, Sedziwosz and many other tried friends were present. Faithful Peter Wysz wearing the miter and carrying the crozier of the bishopric of Krakow, extended his hand in blessing as he conducted service after service.

The guilds had vied with one another in preparing commemorative pageants and merry-making, and for days the teeming city—peasants and nobles, grown-ups and children,—danced and sang and ate and gave thanks together.

Jadwiga, with characteristic generosity, tried to turn the full tribute of the occasion to Jagiello, whose arrival in Poland it commemorated. But how could she? Whose, after all, asked the people, was the real power and whose the delegated? Above all gratitude to the Lithuanian, rose reverent gratitude to herself—their wonderful, valiant queen, hiding her sorrows, effacing herself.

One shadow fell across the scene, though in their love and adoration of Jadwiga many tried on this day to suppress the dark question in their minds: To what future could the new empire look so long as this royal pair remained childless? Others, less sensitive, pressed their questioning—Must there not, after all, exist some secret sin which heaven was thus punishing? However, these were days chiefly of rejoicing, not of questioning. No previous event had so clearly revealed the power of the double throne.

A number of civil and military officials eager to join in the anniversary festival were held in Lithuania, which Witowt had again involved with the Order, this time through negotiations over the Dobryzin lands. He did not even yet realize, as he would later, that he would reach his objective, independent control of Lithuania, not through these temporary alliances with his country's worst enemy, but through further agreements with his cousin, and a complete break with their common foe. In little more than a decade the world was to be thrilled again, as it had been when it watched his and Jagiello's father working together. In the battle of Tannenberg, with the cry "Krakow and Vilno," together these sons were to drive the White Capes at last to utter defeat.

In Witowt, tendencies represented by his father and uncle met. For while standing, as Kiejstut did, for the revival of Lithuanian nationality—under himself he looked, as Olgierd had, toward union with Russia. Following Olgierd's path of diplomacy, he had married his daughter Sophia to Vasily, Grand Duke of Muscovy, and pictured himself as the future liberator of that country through his conquest of the Tatars. Had Jagiello's father, who drove the Horde of Kipchack over the steppes to the Crimea, not been simultaneously engaged with the Order, Lithuania, and not Mucovy, might have become the dominant power of Eastern Europe. Witowt believed he could yet make it that, and already his ear caught the honeyed title "Emperor of the North and the East!" "God prepares me to rule over all lands," he once said.

Jadwiga was not blinded by his grandiose schemes, by his chimerical hopes, and listened with anxiety to his increasing demands for money and supplies—for weapons and horses and harness and experienced leaders. She saw Poland impoverished for ends impossible of attainment, ends which, even could they be achieved, would, through oriental influences, inevitably weaken Slavic civilization. Jagiello lent a more ready ear and hand. Yet he kept his balance and warned and restrained his cousin at many points, encouraging him whenever he thought Witowt's enterprise would fortify the Catholic position of the United Kingdom in Europe.

In this anniversary year, those who foresaw only defeat for Witowt in the East, were obliged to admit his temporary success. For he returned from a victorious campaign with a great number of Tatar prisoners, some of whom he settled in Poland and others in a colony near Vilno. But Jadwiga still saw the Lithuanian wars bringing not benefit but loss to Poland. The only warfare in which the Lithuanian army could really help the United Kingdom was in that against the Order, and except in defense, she was opposed to fighting the Teutonic Knights.

So while ardently continuing her works of peace for both Lithuania and Poland she consistently refused unlimited grants of war supplies to Witowt.

In 1397 she founded a college for Lithuanians in Prague University, something she had long wished to accomplish. She had finally succeeded in buying one of the most beautiful buildings in the Bohemian capital for her purpose—a large house near the palace of King Wenceslaus which fortunately escaped destruction the following year, when so many other buildings were demolished during the religious riots induced by the teachings of John Huss. This school was called the College of Queen Jadwiga. In this year, too, Pope Boniface, of whom Poland had many times asked the privilege of including the faculty of theology in its university to be, granted the request.

Every year now registered additions to Krakow's university site. And more and more Jadwiga was interesting her closest friends among the women of her court in her cherished undertaking. Elizabeth of Meltzyn had been from the beginning her confidante in all plans dear to her heart, and especially in this one for the university. With her, in the "university group," were Constance of Koniecpolska, wife of the governor of Sieradz, Jagiello's sister, Duchess Alexandra of Mazovia, the old Duchess Oteinessa of Pilecka and Katherine Mezykowa of Dabrowy, wife of the Governor of Lvov.

There was many a round-table discussion, when these intelligent, patriotic women gathered about their queen, considered the merits of the Paris university type of organization as contrasted with that of Padua or Bologna. Far-seeing Casimir, who more than thirty years earlier had begun university buildings in the village named after him, outside the city walls, but had not finished them, had followed Bologna. His splendid effort had failed. Jadwiga wished to follow Paris, and, since she could count on the Pope's ever-growing support of her projects, she hoped to include a school of theology with those of law and medicine and philosophy. She planned that handsome buildings in Saint Anne street should serve as living quarters for the faculty. She and her aids talked of teachers to be found, of the number of students to be admitted—of a multitude of things, but oftenest of the library. For the library, Jadwiga believed, was to the university as the spring to the stream.

CHAPTER XXIV

Ambassadress of the Nation

As 1300 drew toward its close, the king, as well as the queen, was increasingly occupied with works of peace. He was superintending the actual purchase of the university properties, pushing the building of churches in Vilno, extending Wawel chateau, and planning to girdle the hill with entirely new fortifications. And he was especially busy in Galicia, encouraging the growth of towns lying to the east of Krakow, further developing the lucrative salt mines of Wieliczka and Bochnia, and the important trade of the city of Lvov. He was an itinerant ruler, doing business on the spot as he visited one after another of his cities or put up at successive royal castles or monasteries. Jadwiga realized now how much her mother had been alone, yet, after all, not alone, for she had had her children.

She, too, was busy abroad, though usually within a narrower radius. One or another of her gilded carriages, with its half dozen horses glistening from their brushing, seemed every few days to be clattering across the courtyard and pulling up at the chateau steps. She did not merely endow monasteries and convents and hospitals, but personally followed their progress, and directed the care of the sick and the poor. One of Krakow's stone masons, to whom she had been kind and whom she one day stopped to praise as he worked, reverently modeled her foot in stone. This sculptured plaque set in the wall of the Carmelite monastery is, today, for Krakovians, a sacred reminder of their debt to their Christian queen.

She frequently visited nearby abbeys and convents to examine their treasure of books before ordering her own. She could not often enough turn the pages of the gorgeous liturgical manuscripts of the Cistercians in Moglia village near the capital, or other famous leaves belonging to the Benedictine brothers at Tyniec. A certain missal with a calendar there, travellers told her, had no equal in any country. One of her own secretaries, the priest, Nicholas Tromba, was a painter of parts, and when he was not overwhelmed with letters to be sent and answered, and with the writing of documents to which with twisted red and green cords he attached the queen's large wax seal, he illustrated for her exquisite little books of hours, copies of sermons, botanies, and other scientific works. She and Jagiello were planning together in memory of his conversion, an elaborate book for one of the new churches in Vilno. It was to have several parts, one to present in glowing words and illuminated picture the coming of the Lord, another the dedication of the church, and a third the gospel of Nicodemus.

Unfortunately, still threatening to undo this work of civilization, loomed the machinations of the Order and the reckless adventuring of Witowt—ironical checkmating—both that of the Order, which had been itself the greatest civilizing agency along the Baltic, and of Witowt, whose enterprises sprang at least partly from his dream of carrying the blessings of the west to the east. Yet despite counter currents, wherever one travelled on the great plains of the Vistula, he heard the noise of hammer and chisel, or encountered some bold trade caravan. A manifold activity testified to the momentum of the forces building the new state.

In France, wrecked by the Hundred Years' War, in Hungary, disintegrating under Sigismund, in Bohemia, weary of the irregularities of Wenceslaus, in Germany, struggling toward unity, in Moscovy, where Duke Vasily, in dread of a Tatar conquest, had ordered from Vladimir to Moscow the miracle-working ikon,—in every court in Europe men watched with astonishment and admiration and envy the progress of the empire on the western frontier. Could they have looked further they would have seen in this progress the dawn of Poland's Golden Age.

Dangers had to be dealt with. The Duke of Oppeln, needing money, had seen in the Order's ambition to possess the Dobryzin lands, his opportunity to rehabilitate himself. So, maintaining that he held this territory independently, and not as a loyal vassal from the crown, he had perilously involved himself with the Knights. A strong party, including the king, greatly aroused by the Order's hold on this northern province, favored war. Some urged it. But Jadwiga still worked unwearyingly to prevent it. So far, she had exhibited an extraordinary skill in calming the ever reborn dispute, winning again and again a peace which she herself feared was but a truce. In this Dobryzin conflict she advocated the method of peaceful negotiation with the same vigor and the same courage which she had shown at another time when she rode at the head of an army to rescue Red Ruthenia. And later, when she made the daring attempt to claim the Árpád inheritance after her sister's death.

Some of those who had witnessed that earlier resoluteness were puzzled by her pacific attitude toward the Order. But others understood that this stand revealed a yet finer quality of courage. It was no easy position to take. She took it because she foresaw the suffering that must desolate her land once the Order's and Poland's armies were in battle. People blessed her for having saved them from that war thus far. Moreover, she still saw on the breast of the Knights, the Cross of Christ, and believed, despite their iniquities, that beneath it must remain something of their earlier spirit. That spirit which had called her father to aid them might even now be moved to see justice. Her influence was so strong that she carried both the king and the nobles with her. And so complete was their confidence in her that they asked her to go in April, 1397, as the Ambassadress of the whole nation, to treat directly with the grand master for the restoration of the occupied Polish lands.

Preliminary interchanges began immediately: envoys hurried between Krakow and Marienburg. The meeting place was agreed upon—one of the Order's fortified castles at Radiec, near the border of the disputed province. Passports were exchanged, Grand Master Conrad von Jungingen's to Queen Jadwiga and her company, hers to the master and his knights. Those to accompany the queen were chosen: first among her political advisers were Sedziwosz of Szubina, governor of Kalisz, and Jasko of Tenczyn, chatelain of Wojnicz; and leading those from her court were Peter Ripska, its head, her chamberlain, Jakusz of Boturzyne, and her master of the table, Jasko of Szezekocina,—then followed an impressive retinue of prelates and magnates.

No effort was spared to make the embassy through its official importance and the splendor of its appearance represent the power of Poland. The journey would be, as usual, not merely a journey, but for the queen, work all along the route. She must conduct a moving court. Whenever she approached a town its officials in their robes of office, and the guilds with their banners, would welcome her at its gates. And at the Cathedral portal the clergy in formal dress would be waiting to lead her amid singing inside. Every great convent along the route was counting on having the holy queen and benefactress under its roof for at least one night, while monasteries competed with cities for that honor. However, during most of the halts a royal castle or hunting lodge would be headquarters.

Krakow had lived through so many thrilling moments since the little girl from Buda arrived, that one might have expected it to be less enthusiastically responsive to new ones than it was. But there was no limit to its interest in anything that touched the most beloved queen. Accustomed as far back as their memories reached to seeing, on an alarm from the north, long lines of steel-clad troops gallop out through the gate, the people were profoundly stirred, as with prayer and singing, they watched the queen and her escort depart on this strange mission.

She passed the first night at the Convent of Our Lord's Tomb in Miechow, and by April twenty-sixth, the company were in Kalisz, where they were guests of the city. No pressure of official duties ever completely took Jadwiga's thoughts from those things which to her were of deepest importance, and here she turned aside to reward her faithful old cook, Dominicus, with the gift of a measure of land in the village of Skotniki. She spent May eighth, the day of Poland's patron saint, Stanislaus, formally celebrated all over the land, in Poznan, where after joining in the religious and civil ceremonies, she remained to assist at the sessions of the royal court of justice, which were attended by high officials from all parts of the province, gathered to welcome her.

At Gnezno, capital of the archbishopric, she was the guest of the archbishop. In the Cathedral where were buried the relics of the martyr, Saint Adalbert, worshipped by the entire Polish people, a magnificent mass was celebrated. And after days which rivalled all the preceding ones in the splendor of their ceremonies, the procession began the last stage of its journey. Another stop at Lada, where the queen made a donation to the Cistercian convent; then at the end of over a month and a half's travelling, they had their first glimpse through the trees, of the towers and walls of the fortress-castle in which success or failure awaited them. From here stretched the possessions of the extraordinary theocracy, each of its twenty districts under a land master and an advisory board of brethren, these masters in turn forming the advisory council of the grand master.

Before they reached the castle, the Poles were welcomed by a company of knights, glorious in white capes and helmets topped with the waving iridescence of peacock feathers, and wearing gleaming, winged spurs. Waiting at the forbidding gateway were Grand Master Conrad, members of his council, the marshal, hospitaller, treasurer, keeper of the wardrobe, and other high officers. They were broad-shouldered, bearded, vigorous men, and wore, too, white capes over their robes and breastplates again emblazoned with the Cross. Others were in less brilliant costumes, and monks added their note of dark simplicity to the scene. Jadwiga's retinue had wished the conference might have been held at the great headquarters, Marienburg, with reports of which the world rang; but they soon saw that this smaller seat had its own beauty of inner court and gothic hall, and outlying buildings. Upon everything it possessed, the Order set the seal of splendor. Despite the fact that parts of Europe were attempting to dethrone the Church, and although the Hundred Years' War and Hussite and other disaffections had already diminished contributions to the White Capes, they were still, in appearance, at the zenith of power. These German builders had demonstrated in their progress toward the control of a territory embracing, as it now did under Conrad, thousands of hamlets and villages, many fortified castles and over half a hundred fortified cities, the power of pageantry and the influence of majestic buildings.

After the queen and her suite had visited the chapel, and refreshed themselves in quarters assigned them, they were escorted to the reception hall, which they found beautiful. Its ceiling held many delicate vaulting ribs sprung from a series of clustered piers running along the middle of the room. In the arched spaces between the corbels were frescoes representing the coronation and other scenes from the life of the holy Virgin for whom Marienburg was named. The stained glass windows presented portrait figures of former grand masters. Painted wooden cabinets stood against the walls and heavy oaken benches and iron-bound chests and tables at the end of the room opposite the grand master's dais, which had a strip of red velvet Brussels carpet before it. Huge logs burned in the open fireplaces and, even though this was the tenth of June, added warmth from the central heating plant below rose through the perforated brass plates set in the patterned marble floor. Below the little upper musicians' balcony ran a row of animal skulls and horns and at various points were other trophies of the chase.

The quick-eyed Poles, as they moved about, missed none of these details. But the thought uppermost in their minds as the scene unrolled was that despite the shining appearance and assurance of Master Conrad and his German soldiers, the impression made by their queen transcended all else. How regal she was in her gold crown with its circling lilies of France, and her ermine-lined crimson velvet mantle. Her severe white robe was ornamented only by the Polish eagle embroidered in white on her breast, and was held above the hips by a broad gold girdle. In her eyes shone the intensity of her purpose. Yet with complete realization of the difficulties before her, she controlled her impatience to drive at once to the point.

A banquet followed the reception, during which an orchestra played in the overhanging balcony. Delicacies from almost every country in Europe were served, while the horn beakers were often refilled with old Rhinewine mixed with eggs and milk. The visitors were amused with wrestling and fencing matches and entertained by singing chroniclers of the

Order. On the following day there would be a tournament in which hosts and guests were to compete.

The diplomatic conversations began the morning after the arrival, prefaced pleasantly by reminiscences of the visits of the queen's father, Louis, Rex Christianissimus, of his sojourns before he started for and after he returned from the crusade against the Lithuanian pagans. Conrad and his soldiers were genuinely moved by this dramatic sequence—Louis' daughter within their gates! If she had but come on other business!

For while they honored and reverenced her both for her father's sake and for her own long, patient intervention on their behalf, they had from the beginning no thought of yielding except in appearance to her demand. They would never part with occupied Dobryzin territory—they had the Holy Roman Emperor's support in their possession of it—or with any other land, except at the point of the sword. Still arrogantly confident, they saw no sword breaking their own.

At the end of several days' argument, Conrad offered to remind Oppeln that he held his lands as a vassal of Poland! Further, he agreed to restore certain portions of the Dobryzin if Poland would pay the Order 40,000 florins, loaned, he held, when the land was taken as security. That was the best he could do.

All present knew that this proposition was but veiled refusal. Jadwiga had been fighting with extraordinary energy and diplomatic skill. Realizing that this was probably her last great opportunity in the battle which she had believed, for so long, she might eventually win, she returned again and again to the field after it appeared lost. In the end, lifting her hand as she faced Conrad, in a voice in which the note of prophecy mingled with bitterness and sadness, she cried, "So long as I live the crown will endure your iniquities, but after my death the chastisement of heaven will fall upon you, and then inevitable war will consummate your ruin!"

She turned back heavy-heartedly toward Krakow. Yet she still refused to believe that the door had completely shut: she would continue her struggle, however hopeless it might seem, to shield her people from war. Despite the failure of her mission, after her return, according to custom, she sent gifts to the grand Master in recognition of his hospitality, among them three unusually fine mushrooms.

During the remainder of this year and the succeeding one, letter dates reveal how busy the queen kept Tromba and other secretaries. She tried to gain her objective first by one path, then by another, as she persistently repeated her demand. As 1398 advanced, no messenger rode through Wawel Gate more frequently than the knight wearing the tuft of peacock plumes on his helmet and carrying in his leather saddle bag a parchment to which was attached Conrad's heavy wax seal. On the royal desk, the communications in but one little packet bore the dates,

March 30th, April 15th, May, June, July 2nd, August 4th.

When the grand master was not writing about the Dobryzin land controversy, he was asking for a lowering of Krakow's customs duties, or complaining against some obstructionist act of its commercial agents, which interfered with the Order's caravans plying back and forth across Poland.

Jadwiga's world-heralded, moving effort had its intimate personal angle. Whenever the Order troubled him, Jagiello could not control his bitter impatience with his wife, and her group of pacifist seigneurs. Which helped to widen the breach made by their differences regarding crown lands and support of Witowt. There were rumors that sharp words and neglect caused the queen much unhappiness. But we hear no words of her own confirming such reports. There was loneliness, that, all knew, but if the king made her suffer, she concealed that fact beneath a control and dignity which had never yet deserted her. To chroniclers, who saw her work in perspective, she appeared more and more exalted, her self-immolation increasingly sublime. "White dove of the ark," one wrote, "who held the trembling olive branch above the mounting tides of passion and hate."

In '98 Prince Witowt, fighting some two hundred miles beyond Vilno, won another great Tatar victory. This made it still more difficult for the queen to stand firmly against support of the eastern wars, in which she still foresaw inevitable ultimate defeat.

How much already had Witowt's wars cost Poland? She had withheld grants when she could, and prevented many Poles from going off with him to the steppes.

It was with a feeling of sadness and impotence that she saw Witowt, now strong and independent in Lithuania, receive from Jagiello part of Podolia which had come to the Polish crown under Casimir. Then she took a bold, but considered step; she wrote Witowt, whose goal was independent control of Lithuania, asking him to pay, on crown lands in his possession, the taxes of a loyal vassal! Some gasped; many did not conceal their misgivings as to the consequences of this demand—might not Witowt turn once again to the Order? Others believed him too deeply engaged in Russia to treat the matter as seriously as he would have at another time. In the Senate, which he convened, after reading the Queen's letter, he asked if any one had ever heard that Lithuania or Samogitia had paid tribute to Poland. "No!" came the expected cry. Thus supported at home, and by the Order abroad, he again gave his attention to Tatar war plans.

Sigismund's visit at the end of the year offered pleasant relief from controversy. Both sovereigns were eager to make his reception outshine if possible preceding ones, and it seemed to; for during their reign Wawel courtyard had not witnessed a more splendid series of tourneys. They attracted gay knights and ladies from far and near. On the first day, twenty knights in green and in steel armor were conducted to the lists by twenty ladies in green and silver robes, each riding a beautiful horse and leading her knight by ribbons of her chosen colors. At supper the fortunate lady awarded the prize to the victor. After several days of jousts and balls, Sigismund returned happily to Hungary carrying with him his many gifts.

Then, as the last year of the century approached, suddenly for Jadwiga the whole world was changed.

CHAPTER XXV

Birth and Death

Queen Jadwiga's concern about Witowt and the Order—all thoughts but one—were crowded to the periphery of her mind. A song filled her days; she was on her knees in a very ecstasy of thanksgiving. Perhaps there was an explanation of the bitter years of barrenness in the significant time of her annunciation, some mystical meaning in this coming of her child just as the new century dawned. She prayed for forgiveness for her sin of impatience.

The king, in a transport of joy, sent the news far and wide; it ran along the rivers and across the plains like a wind. Hungary was scarcely less jubilant than Poland, in every court of Europe there was rejoicing—except at Marienburg! A Te Deum was sung in Rome and the Pope wrote a letter of congratulation asking that he might give his name to the child, and designating, since he feared he could not be present, the celebrated scoliast and papal nuncio for Poland, Adalbert Jastrzobiec, as his representative who would hold the baby at the baptismal font.

Mass was celebrated in every church in the United Kingdom. While in Wawel Cathedral, where on the day of her arrival Jadwiga had knelt, a young girl, before the high altar, and where since then the seal had been set upon each successive dramatic event in her experience, the great of the realm gathered and three masses in succession were sung. Polish warriors returned gloriously from the marches, Lithuanian boyars wearing not one, but three or four embroidered mantles to honor the occasion, Ruthenian princes in robes of stiff gold worked with Byzantine effigies, powerful burghers, brilliantly dressed wives of governors and other officials, ambassadors from foreign courts,—all rendered homage as the king walked from the sacristy to the altar. A few moments later Queen Jadwiga followed. Tall and more beautiful than ever, she scarcely showed the promise of maternity as she walked down the nave holding her missal. She wore no jewels except those adorning her rosary. That there was nothing perfunctory about this service, the fervent responses proved; what love, what gladness for her and for Poland filled the place!

After mass the queen withdrew to her apartment while the king entertained his guests at luncheon, placing at his right the papal nuncio, and at his left Bishop Peter. Later in the afternoon Jadwiga received the wives of the governors, Duchess Alexandra and a large number of other women, all burning to talk and plan with her—the court had plunged into a protracted competition in sewing and embroidering! Elizabeth had come first, before the more formal hour, to throw her arms about her darling friend. She was a sister in those days, when Jadwiga so longed for her mother or Mary,—for at least one of her family to share her happiness. Besides giving an enfolding affection, Elizabeth, out of her full experience —she had now five children—was daily giving her friend practical counsel. She often brought exquisite little Jadwiga with her to play about while she talked with the royal godmother.

In all the planning Jadwiga insisted on simplicity; everything should be lovely, yes, but nothing elaborate. She had been living more and more as a nun, and even in her new joy the reaction from long suffering made her want to prove by increased self-denial her passionate gratitude to heaven. She was living so rigorously that she may, without realising it, have weakened her resistance.

The baby was expected in July, but months in advance people began to prepare, especially at Buda, to make the journey to Krakow to be present at this baptism for which history had so long waited. They sent gifts ahead, not willing to wait until the customary time of presentation.

Jagiello, once he had given release to his emotion in announcements and plans, went away again to towns east of Krakow. But vigilant Bishop Peter was never far away. Knowing how greatly the thought of any death sentence or bloodshed made the queen suffer, he prevented the condemnation of Zysko, and helped to influence the capital to avoid any executions during her pregnancy. He even counseled her against overdoing, in her mystic fervor, the hours of fasting and meditation and prayer.

Remembering her father, people had not been surprised at Jadwiga's growing asceticism. She was, to be sure, much younger than he, when he had wished for monastic seclusion. But experience had conspired to advance in her the desire for such a period of withdrawal. Each year suffering had further stressed the profound truth of Scribe John's earlier teaching that life's bright objective is the complete gift of itself to others.

Such goodness as hers never needed explanation; instinctively the people knew her heart. Nor was it strange that their reverent love for her and faith in her should flower in a reputation for "cures." Paralytics declared themselves well after they had been touched by her hand. Many among the simpler people held her to be a saint. One incident alone, that of the saving of the coppersmith's son, reported far and wide, was sufficient to spread belief in her miraculous powers. On Corpus Christi Day, during the religious celebration in which she participated, the son of a coppersmith fell into the river and was drowned. Queen Jadwiga quickly left the procession and kneeling beside the inert little body, threw her silk mantle over it. Soon the weeping mother felt her boy's hand grow warm in her own and making the sign of the Cross, she cried out that a miracle had been performed. From that time, when any member of their craft died, the guild of coppersmiths threw a silken mantle over the coffin.

In this century of presences and powers, districts sent deputations to the holy queen to win through her rain or fair weather, to appeal for tufted hay and full honeycombs. Were there ever so many fish, they asked, in the lakes, or was there ever so much game in the forest as during this the closing year of the century, blessed by her expectancy? Chroniclers in far courts reported that because of her "barons whose hatred ravaged the frontier released their captives and restored the herds they had seized; that her benevolence softened the fate of slaves, the pride of masters, the rigor of judges."

In her aloneness, for no matter how devoted were her ladies in waiting and matrons of honor and Bishop Peter and Knight Jasko and others, she was alone, this love and confidence must have been precious. However heroic in her self-effacement, she must yet have leaned gratefully upon it. Now those who had formerly appealed to her and drawn comfort from her were rejoicing with her. They set their candles and flickering wicks before shrines from one border of the land to the other.

Already in early June Krakow rumbled with visitors. Its convents and monasteries and hospitable palaces and inns were being taxed to their limit to house the companies daily bearing in through the gates. In the market place and at street corners groups of warriors and gentlemen, who had travelled far, monks and nuns from foundations owing their existence to the holy queen's generosity and chroniclers who would miss no preliminaries to the great event, exchanged bits of news from the chateau. They discussed not only the gifts they had brought but those they counted on carrying away with them, for King Jagiello's reputation for generosity was established. Interest centered on the expected arrival of the neighboring kings, Wenceslaus and Sigismund. Sigismund was not popular, but his naïve enjoyment of any celebration, especially of one in which he starred, as he would as brother-in-law, in this one, pleased the city. His presence would help to make up for dashing Prince Witowt's absence—Witowt was in desperate battle with the Tatars on the Lower Dnieper. His gift was the handsomest so far received, an exquisitely wrought silver cradle. People liked to think of it waiting in its beauty near the royal bed.

They especially liked thinking of the silver cradle because they knew that the queen had refused to prepare her chamber for the birth day in the customary luxurious manner. Not long before, King Jagiello had, in an excited letter, asked her to have the walls hung with the most splendid brocades and tapestries procurable and to spread her bed with jewelled coverings. But this she refused to do, replying that she had not renounced the world's glitter and pomp only to call it back in this solemn hour.

When the report spread that the hour of delivery seemed near and the king had not yet arrived from eastern Galicia, there was consternation—a courier flew with the tidings. Bishop Peter was constantly at the queen's bedside. Anna and Elizabeth were always near. She was given soups brewed from sustaining herbs. People hurried to the churches, lighted a myriad candles and on their knees awaited the announcement. Others knelt in the streets, while crowds encircled Wawel Hill. When on June 22nd, the word came, shouts of relief and joy echoed in nave and transcept and from city wall to wall. But soon afterward, in many eyes appeared a look of anxiety—reports from the chamber said that the baby was weak, perhaps even ill. However, the fact that there was no indication of a postponement of any part of the festival program was reassuring.

In the Cathedral, the very next day, before witnesses representing a large part of Europe, the first baptism of the great Jagiellonian dynasty was celebrated. The papal nuncio held the baby, in whose tiny body flowed the blood of Piasts and Anjevins and the line of Gedymin. It was christened Elizabeth Bonifacia—after Jadwiga's mother, and for the Pope.

Succeeding festivities were not to continue long. Cutting like a sword across them came the word that Jadwiga's baby and the heir to the throne was dead. The king after breathless riding, had arrived only to see his hope perish. Joy was turned into mourning and visitors sadly prepared to start homeward.

People dared not think of the queen. What to do? So long as possible the news must be kept from her, but for how long could it be? Tragically soon, Bishop Peter read in her eyes as she lay still in her chamber, her hair enwreathing her white face like a halo, her hands clasping the crucifix, that she divined the truth from which all were trying to shield her. She turned pathetically toward the little travelling altar piece on the stand beside her bed, the one she had brought with her from Buda, as if calling on Buda—on mother, sister, to help her now. She asked that the window be kept open that she might see the blue sky during the day and the stars at night.

Then rallying, her mind was actively occupied with important state matters. She and Jagiello discussed their cherished university plan, now happily so near realization. Could she but have seen this university, her supreme legacy, living through the ages, as her posthumous child, agent of faith and civilization, adding with each century of service a new glory to the halo the people were to set above her name, she might have felt sweet comfort.

Witowt's adventure, on the other hand, was going badly, as she had always felt that in the end it must. She reiterated her opposition to Poland's support of the Tatar wars. Often she returned to the subject of the king's status in their double reign—wishing to clear up beyond question any uncertainty regarding his title. And one afternoon, quietly facing death, she asked him, in case she should not recover, to marry Anna, daughter of the Piast noble Count Cilly of Hungary; this marriage would further secure his position. He promised, though he saw her premonitory request as but a natural result of her condition—after a few weeks of rest she would be again at Court. So he thought, as he prepared to return to his work in cities east of Krakow.

Elizabeth, who inwardly had never been reconciled to the great renunciation, asked bitterly now if William would have thus left her beloved friend to bear her grief alone. If Jadwiga herself ever asked that question she would never know. Bishop Peter's fears were not so easily quieted as the king's, nor were faithful Knight Jasko's. They were never long absent from the chateau and increasingly at the royal bedside. With hearts torn by pity, they realized that the queen, after her valiant summoning of energy from some hidden reserve, as she planned with the king for Poland's future, had relapsed into alarming weakness. Seeing her strength swiftly ebbing, and sensing her effort to compose her soul, they tried to cheer her, to support her tired spirit, reporting all news they thought might turn her mind back toward life.

During one of these hours the queen interrupted them. "If I should die," she said, "it must be you two most proven, most loyal friends who will execute my wishes. My will is simple: one half of the proceeds of the sale of all that I have, jewels, clothes, ornaments, possessions of every kind, I leave to the University of Krakow, and the other half to be divided among the poor. Little must be spent on funeral ceremonies. I wish no elaborate service or eulogy, no monument of any kind. Let my body be placed beside that of my baby on the gospel side of the altar, with a plain inscription on the facing marble to mark the place."

So, once again, this time supremely, as they knelt in reverent adoration beside her, she revealed to them the greatness of her soul. Still they endeavored to convince her that life, not death, was before her. How young, how beautiful, how utterly, utterly alone! One by one those she had loved and touched had been taken from her, yet her faith was undimmed. Was God demonstrating to the world through her victory the strength of the spirit which leans upon him?

Alarming reports spread across the city below, when, the second time during a month, a messenger was dispatched to summon the king in all haste. The women of the court who had watched the buoyant, radiant girl from Buda grow to more radiant young womanhood, had held all along to the hope that one morning they would find a return of that vitality. But now she had asked for extreme unction and was calling them one by one to bid them farewell.

The papal nuncio, and highest members of the clergy and officials of the court gathered in the vaulted chamber, others in the corridor, and beyond them her cook, and those who had longest and most intimately served her. Anna and Elizabeth knelt at the foot of the bed and Bishop Peter and Knight Jasko beside it. And as white robed nuns held the lighted candles a little nearer, and the nuncio placed the crucifix more comfortably in the queen's hands, the soft chanting of the prayers for the dying began—repeated below the hill, as the morning lengthened toward noon, by the whole city on its knees.

Those who on entering the chamber were unable to control their sobbing found themselves suddenly comforted—so marvelous was the quietness and resignation in the beautiful pale face on the pillow. From it a light, as of white peace, seemed almost to illumine the room. Then about noontime, while the chanting continued, suddenly the queen lifted her hand and smiled as if in farewell, and all knew that she had gone. They passed in procession to kneel and kiss the still hand on the coverlid.

The black flag with the white skull and two crossed tibias was swiftly raised over the chateau. The king saw it miles away, long before he galloped, dust covered, and with bitter realization now, through the gate and up the hillside—too late!

On the day of her death, July 17, 1399, Krakow inscribed the following words in the city's Latin calendar: "Today, at noon, died Jadwiga, Queen of Poland—unwearied creator of divine culture, protectress of the Church, administrator of justice, servant of all virtues, humble and beneficent mother of orphans, who in her time has had no equal of royal blood in the eyes of men in the whole world."

The body lay in state four weeks while Poland mourned before it. In every court in Europe—including that of the Order—a Mass was said for the repose of the holy queen's soul. Then, on the fourteenth of August, in the last year of the century, after the royal pomp of the final funeral service and ovation, Jadwiga was buried, with her baby, in the simplest manner, as she had requested, on the Gospel side of the altar. There they lie today, and not, as many believe, beneath the recumbent figure of the queen which now adds its loveliness to the ancient nave.

Jagiello had wished at once to erect such a monument, but respecting Jadwiga's wishes, had only the simple record of her name and dates inscribed on the oblong of dark green marble sealing her burial place. Indeed, the king seemed to the end of his days to try to carry out Jadwiga's wishes. He did not die until he had passed eighty,—from a cold caught, it was said, in a forest while listening to a nightingale. After Jadwiga's death, William married, but he lived scarcely a half dozen years longer than she.

Every day brought further proof of Jadwiga's foresight and wisdom. But a few days after her burial, Witowt, after suffering disastrous defeat on the lower Dnieper, escaped from the "blood bath of Worskla" only because of his swift horse. At the dedication of the university, the following year, her spirit reigned. And at critical moments in his continuing struggle with the German Knights, Jagiello seemed to be listening to her counsel. The day she foresaw arrived, when with Witowt, at Tannenberg, in 1410, he broke their power. He married Anna, as she had asked, and was twice married afterwards, but it was her wedding ring which he cherished to the end.

Buried on Wawel Hill, yet what a living presence Jadwiga is in the country whose fate destiny placed in her brave young hands five hundred years ago. Her people cleave to her, distilling from her ardent youth a golden quality which enriches their own, and from her years of wisdom and holiness an essence which vitalizes the very source of their national idealism. The evolution of her spirit is in itself a fascinating story—a story which will end only when Poland ends.

INDEX

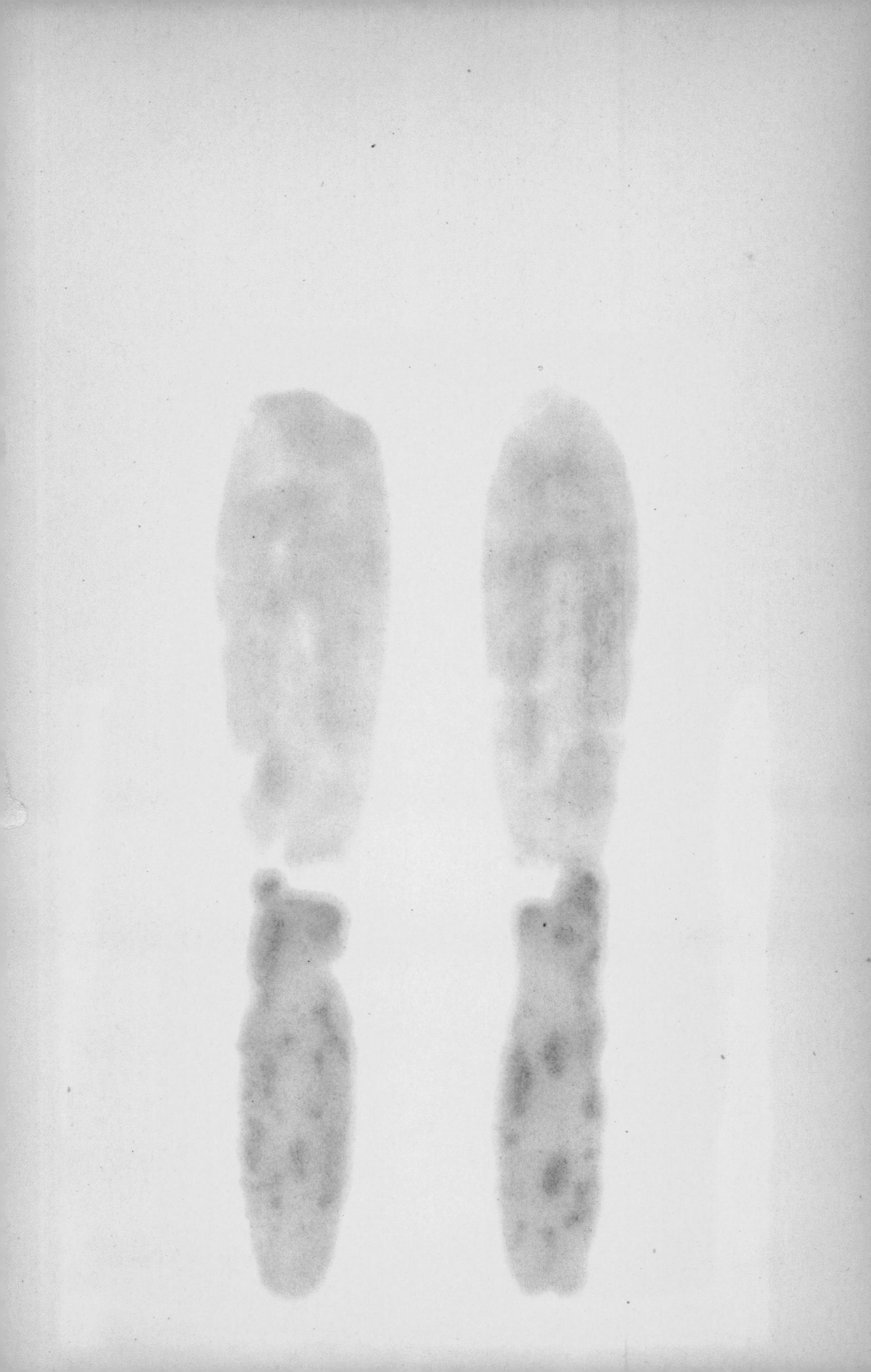